HARRY POTTER,
YOU'RE THE BEST!

HARRY POTTER,
You're the Best!

 A TRIBUTE FROM FANS THE WORLD OVER

SHARON MOORE

 St. Martin's Griffin 🞄 New York

www.stmartins.com

Design by Kate Nichols

Library of Congress Cataloging-in-Publication Data

Harry Potter, you're the best! : a tribute from fans the world over /
[edited by] Sharon Moore.—1st ed.
        p.   cm.
    ISBN 0-312-28254-0
    1. Rowling, J. K.—Characters—Harry Potter.   2. Potter, Harry
    (Fictitious character)   3. Children's stories, English—Appreciation.
    4. Fantasy fiction, English—Appreciation.   5. Wizards in literature.
    6. Magic in literature.   I. Moore, Sharon.   II. Title.

PR6068.O93 Z7 2001
823'.914—dc21   2001031945

First Edition: September 2001

10   9   8   7   6   5   4   3   2   1

To Ian Moore, *myth-master*

To David Moore, *musical magician*

   and

To Joyce Moore, Jenifer Ross, and Chris Wilcox,

literary wizards at City Lights Bookstore in

Sylva, North Carolina

Contents

List of Illustrations

Introduction:
The Magic of Imagination

Harry Potter fans have been through a lot in the recent past. You have encountered the Dark Mark, the Tri-wizard Tournament, Mad-Eye Moody, the Death Eaters, and Harry's duel with Lord Voldemort, to name just a few of your hero's adventures.

Like Harry, you learned a lot as you struggled through these scary moments. In the letters you have sent us, you told us that you are reading more and more. Your letters show that you are learning to write well, too!

The comments you've shared with us, which we are publishing here, are very thoughtful and expressive. Some describe strong emotions. Others show what great senses of humor you have.

Many of you wrote that you were inspired by reading what other children had to say in our previous volume, *We Love Harry Potter!*, published by St. Martin's Press in 1999. And now, with our present book, Harry Potter has achieved another magical triumph—he has enabled children from all over the world to communicate with each other.

Something else we learn from reading the Harry Potter books is that there is a strong connection between the words "magic" and "imagination." It takes a lot of imagination to create magic,

and since children have imagination aplenty you take great pleasure in the magic of J. K. Rowling's writing. The creativity in her books encourages you, her readers, to try making literary magic of your own. And you have! A great many of you said that you plan to become writers yourselves, "just like J. K. Rowling."

Reading itself is a kind of magic. It enables us to see things that are not really there but that are represented by words. In the Harry Potter books, J. K. Rowling has created pictures for our minds that can be produced only by words. We can identify with Harry's unhappy home life with the Dursleys, understand Hermione's bossiness, and feel the contentment of the Weasley household because of the way the author describes them. Different readers see different pictures in their minds when they read the stories. That means that each of you has your own personal friendships with the books, and gradually the books become an important part of your life. And to think that books are made only of paper and ink!

Some of you told us how old you were when you wrote to us, and some did not. That's why the ages of only some of the contributors are included in this book.

One topic was mentioned so frequently by you that it deserves to be addressed right here and now. That topic is the pronunciation of Hermione's name. According to Ms. Rowling, the name is pronounced "her-MY-uh-nee."

Many other children were mystified by the identity of the old man on the back cover of the first Harry Potter book. This is not surprising. By the time you've finished reading the book you've met so many mysterious characters that it's hard to imagine which one—besides Harry—should be depicted on the cover. But the answer is given quite clearly, I think, at the bottom of page 8 of that book, and on page 126 (in the Letters from the Classroom chapter) of this book.

And, finally, here's a salute to all you charming and talented children whose work makes up this book. May we all meet next year at Hogwarts!

—SHARON MOORE

HARRY POTTER,
YOU'RE THE BEST!

1

What We Like (or Dislike) About the Books:

What's So Special About Them?

There are about as many reasons to like the Harry Potter books as there are readers of them. The books appeal to children of all ages from all over the world; the letters in this book were written by children six to nineteen years old, from wherever the English language is spoken, read, or studied. For a lot of kids, the Harry Potter books are a family affair, shared by siblings and parents. More and more children have become interested in writing themselves, thanks to these books. To them, J. K. Rowling is a real-life heroine, and they express their enthusiasm in the letters that follow.

*

Avery, *Santa Ana, California*

The reason I like Harry Potter's adventures is because there are so many surprises. The Dursleys are so mean to Harry, but I guess that there are those kinds of people in the world, and we have to live with it.

I wish that I could go to Hogwarts and learn magic. I guess that we have a kind of magic in the Muggle world, like growing

plants, making fire, and things like that, so I guess no one is really a Muggle.

I would like to tell Harry to take more magic classes to get stronger so he can maybe defeat Voldemort. But he doesn't have to if he doesn't want to, because I know it's hard to have so much homework and stress.

✳

Heather, *Sudbury, Ontario, Canada*

I bet that Hogwarts would be extremely fun. I would hate summer vacation because you can't use magic (and the Dursleys are completely dumb)! Quidditch must be amazing. If I could play, I would be a Seeker just like Harry, because I like looking for things. I wish we could play it in the Muggle world, but that would be impossible!

Harry is lucky to have an owl! If I could have any pet, I would get a snowy owl like Hedwig and an orange cat like Hermione's cat, Crookshanks.

I wish that Harry Potter could write to me, but he would have to use Muggle post, because I don't think my parents would appreciate an owl flying through the house!

∗

Bianca, *Perth, Australia, 10½ years old*

I love reading and I can't put the Harry Potter books down. Most of my friends have started to pick up the books from libraries. It is very good at our school because there are lots of copies. Lots of people pick up the books at reading time.

Although the people in the books are very different from us, the books show Harry's life as a kid in our world's point of view. I also found that everyone's thoughts were captured well.

I don't think that Harry's parents lived in the Muggle world, because they were great friends of Albus Dumbledore, and so I think they must have lived somewhere like the Weasleys.

∗

Lindsey, *Port Chester, New York, 9 years old*

I like Harry Potter because he is sort of not alert when things are about to happen in real life.

I got my mom into reading the Harry Potter books. We miss reading them, now that we have read them all. I wonder what happened to You-Know-Who? Every time I say that to my mom she cracks up. One time she was rolling on the floor, she was giggling so hard.

When I walk past a window and see a little boy or girl reading a Harry Potter book, it makes me happy inside. I say in my mind, "Oh, she or he is going to have fun reading that book. It's going to take her inside her own world."

There should be a TV series called *Harry Potter and Friends,* with a chapter for one whole hour, and then it would say, "to be continued." It should actually be an Imax TV series cartoon.

∗

Annamarie, *Heap Bridge, Bury, England, 10 years old*

I absolutely adore the Harry Potter books! If J. K. Rowling's wonderful effort hadn't been put into the whole four books, I don't think any child or adult or grandma and granddad would've made the effort to read them. And I just want to tell her that she shouldn't stop there at her seventh book, no siree! She should carry on and carry on so the Harry Potter legend lives on!

I'd love to be in Harry's family, like his little brother or sister and go on all his adventures with him.

I've got two sisters, Susanne and Catherine (we're triplets!), and they would love to meet Harry, Ron, and Hermione. We would all help write the best books ever! We'll all use our imaginations. But, you know, it might just be true! You know what, I think it *is* true!

*

Brittany, *Laredo, Texas, 10 years old*

Harry Potter is a good book for just reading. When you go into a bookstore, the thing that goes through your mind is, "Why are we doing this?" After the purchase, you're saying, "It was worth it."

When you go into the bookstore and ask for *Harry Potter and the Goblet of Fire,* for a few minutes you are tense. You think, "Will I like this book?" Your palms start to sweat. Your hair is damp. (Nerve-wrecking, isn't it?) Your feet go numb.

And, finally, they bring out the books. You grasp one and go to the counter. There's a lady in front if you. She has a camera, and she has a book bag. She asks to take your picture. You go red in the face. Your hands are shaking with excitement as you walk out with your book.

That's how I felt getting the fourth Harry Potter book.

*

Ashley, *New Fairfield, Connecticut*

I went to New York City and got J. K. Rowling's autograph. She looked very nice. It was *sooo* cold outside that my dad and I had to go into an Old Navy store and get another coat for me and some hot chocolate.

I have read all of the books eight times. I'm letting my teacher borrow my Harry Potter books, and she enjoys them a lot, too!

*

Joanna, *Massapequa, New York, 11 years old*

I have a special group of friends who are separate from my regular friends. They are fun to be with, but they are slightly different. They are wizards—Harry Potter, Hermione Granger, and Ron Weasley. I have adventures and study at a wizarding school, just by reading four magnificent books.

These books are so lifelike that when I read them, I am a wizard. I fight the evil Voldemort, and I discover dragons, three-headed dogs, and other strange things. J. K. Rowling must have had these experiences. But wait, she couldn't have! It's her unique style of writing that captures children's and adults' imaginations.

When I read these books I laugh, cry, and smile at different parts. I talk about these books and characters with my regular friends. At one time, I even wished to meet them.

I don't know how J. K. Rowling comes up with these beautifully written books, but they are definitely masterpieces.

*

Jo, *Landsborough, Australia*

I think the Harry Potter books are great! After morning tea our whole class reads it. We are up to the third book. Our class has been looking up Harry Potter on the Internet. I can't wait until the fifth book comes out and the movie comes out.

*

Allison, *West Chicago, Illinois*

The Harry Potter books are the best books on earth! I finished the fourth one over the summer. I could never guess what happened at the end. Could you? The name of the last chapter, "The Beginning," really explains a lot.

I'm not a fan, I'm a fanatic!

✳

Jude, *Houma, Louisiana*

I wish I had magic powers like Harry Potter. It must be cool to change people into toads or slugs.

Quidditch is awesome! I would like to play it, but I'm not a wizard. I wonder if now that Harry has his Firebolt maybe he could let me have his Nimbus Two Thousand?

It must be hard for a wizard to live with Muggles. A wizard could put a spell on them to make them fat and ugly, but it probably would not work because they are already as fat and ugly as they can be!

✳

Courtney, *Peach Bottom, Pennsylvania, 11 years old*

I really like the part in book one when Harry first figures out that he's a wizard. I bet he was jumping up and down when Hagrid told him he was going to leave the Dursleys and go to Hogwarts. My mom said that I'm going to get the whole Harry Potter series when they all come out! Yay! I have a few posters with Harry on them hanging in my room and the little book called *We Love Harry Potter!* I think that when Harry is an adult, he'll be the greatest wizard of all!

✳

Amanda, *St. Louis, Missouri, 18 years old*

I guess I should introduce myself. My name is Amanda. A lot of people call me Mandy and that's okay with me. I will be turning nineteen soon.

I really like J. K. Rowling's books. I would love to be a writer, too, but my stories are always so dull. I found a biography of Ms. Rowling in the library at school. I love to read, also. Do you think I will ever become a writer? I guess I just need a good subject to write about, to make a good beginning like Ms. Rowling's first book.

*

Samantha, *Banbury, Oxfordshire, England*

I have two best friends. One of them absolutely loves Harry Potter books and simply can't put them down. The other friend hates them and wouldn't be seen anywhere near a Harry Potter book. At first I agreed with the friend who hates them. The reason was, I had never tried one. My other best friend managed to persuade me to try one. I simply couldn't put it down! It took me two weeks to read books one to four. I was obsessed with them and I wouldn't stop talking about all the exciting adventures of Harry Potter. If I could have any wish, it would be to turn into a witch. Not an ugly witch, but one in J. K. Rowling's stories.

*

Morgan, *Loveland, Colorado, 11 years old*

I think the first Harry Potter book was the best, because that is when I first met Harry, Hermione, and Ron. I read it at my cousins' house. They wanted me to come and play Guns with them but I said, "Later."

*

Louise, *Airdrie, Scotland, 13 years old*

I live very near Edinburgh, where Joanne Rowling wrote her Harry Potter books. Her fantastic books seem just as popular over in the States as they are here! I am a huge fan of these books, even though I never expected to be, as I read the third book first. I am quite an advanced reader and I read it one day for fun. I didn't realize I was about to read the best story ever put down on paper! I rushed straight out to my local bookshop and bought the first two. I waited on tenterhooks for the fourth book. I got it the day it came out, and finished it the next.

Joanne Rowling makes a completely ridiculous story line sound believable and interesting. I think she must be incredibly smart to write such wonderful books.

✳

Kelly, *Frederick, Maryland, 8 years old*

I like all the books so far, especially in the third book at the end when Harry and Hermione go back in time. My mom reads them to me at night. I got my dad into them, and when I was asleep he took them to read.

Fred and George are funny. I liked what they said at Christmas, "Why do our sweaters have an F and G on them? We know our names are Gred and Forge."

I hope that the books keep linking together and being unpredictable.

✳

Dougie, *Columbus, Ohio, 9 years old*

I love reading the Harry Potter stories with my mom. She really likes them, too. I wish I could make my potions as good as Hermione's. She must study really hard at Hogwarts to be so smart. I wonder if they have special birthday parties at Hogwarts?

✳

Ashley, *Indianola, Iowa*

The Harry Potter books are great. They give you something to think about.

I would like to ask J. K. Rowling a few questions. I am going to try to guess her name. Is it Jennifer Kathrine Rowling or Jacky

Katie Rowling? Did she ever go on vacations as a kid? What state did she live in as a kid? Did she read a lot as a kid? What part does she think she would be good at in Quidditch? I think it would be fun to play Quidditch. I would be good at Seeker, because I am skinny and light.

> ➡ *Note: Author Rowling's name is Joanne Kathleen and her friends call her Jo. She grew up in Edinburgh, Scotland, and she still lives there. She did read a lot as a kid, and she still does. She wrote her first story when she was six.*

✶

Grainne, *County Galway, Ireland, 12 years old*

J. K. Rowling is an inspiration to me as I too hope to be a great writer one day. I have already saved up for the third and fourth books. I would like to thank her for giving the children of the world the great gift of her imagination.

✶

Jordan, *Meriden, Connecticut, 8 years old*

Before the Harry Potter books came out I was totally bored. But now, I love to read! If or when J. K. Rowling retires, her books will probably be the most popular books in these United States.

✶

Terri, *Pontypool, Wales, 15 years old*

I just finished the fourth book. A lot of my friends have never read *Harry Potter*, as it wasn't around when we were young enough to get into it, but now I own all the books! I just can't put them down. I dressed up as Harry during my work experience, and I read the first three books to children, to help advertise the fourth one.

I hope more people start reading the books! (You're never too young . . . or old!)

★

Emily, *Jupiter, Florida, 12 years old*

I read *We Love Harry Potter!* and I thought it was a great idea to ask kids what they thought of Harry Potter. Not only does it inform *Harry Potter* readers about what other dedicated fans think but also it can persuade people to read the Harry Potter series.

I am one of those people who read naturally. Many of my friends do not read books on a daily basis but were thrilled by Harry Potter after they first started reading the books. Adults are picking up on the Harry Potter craze, too.

My favorite character is Hermione because she reminds me of my friend Lindsay Baker, smart and always at work.

The Harry books, I assure you, are not a passing fad. J. K. Rowling wrote a masterpiece. These books won't be forgotten soon.

★

Margaret, *London, Ontario, Canada*

Harry Potter books are the best. The characters are great (except for the ones Harry doesn't like). The books aren't like any other book because there are funny parts, scary parts, happy parts, and best of all—suspense!

★

Bo, *Algonquin, Illinois, 9 years old*

At first I thought *Harry Potter* sounded like a stupid kind of fantasy. Then my friend let me borrow the first Harry Potter book. I liked it so much I couldn't stop reading! I wonder why everybody is afraid of saying Voldemort's name? I don't mind it myself. *Voldemort, Voldemort . . .* Well, that's enough of that.

I especially like the endings of the books. It was so exciting at the end of *Harry Potter and the Sorcerer's Stone!*

When I finished the first book I said, "I can't believe I finished it in three days!" Then my friend let me borrow the second one. The same thing happened to me with the second book. I couldn't stop reading. When my mom called me for dinner I said, "Let me just finish this page." After I finished I was so desperate to find out what happens next I just kept reading.

I finished *Harry Potter and the Chamber of Secrets* in three days, too. When I found out that my friend didn't have the third book I was so disappointed. I told my dad, and two days later we went to Borders bookstore and ended up with all three books. Guess what happened to me on the third one, too? Yep, I couldn't stop.

The Harry Potter books are the best books I ever read.

∗

Christopher, *Woodbury, Minnesota, 12 years old*

I have read the whole Harry Potter series five times. I was even Harry Potter for Halloween. The books are as good as a Popsicle on a hot day! I like to write stories, too.

I think the character of Harry Potter is a good role model for children because he knows the difference between good and evil. He is very brave and he treats his friends with respect.

When I read the books I can picture exactly what everyone looks like and what everyone is doing.

My mom has to pry the books out of my hands when I go to bed at night. (She has read all the books, too.) People say I even look a little like Harry Potter!

I am going to keep all the books and one day give them to my children to read.

∗

Ewan, *Wallington, Surrey, England*

I myself am a Christian, and I do not understand why a Christian school banned the Harry Potter books; even my minister reads them! The school says they are un-Christian. Harry Potter books are like the Bible, though—good against evil—and to all the tiniest details. If I were in that school, I personally would disobey that rule to the full extent.

I noticed, well, my mum did, that Remus Lupin is a very interesting name indeed. It is Latin. Remus is taken from Romulus and Remus, the founders of Rome, who were in fact raised by wolves. "Moony" is Lupin's nickname, because he is a werewolf, and a werewolf changes at the full moon; also, *lupus* is Latin for "wolf." "Padfoot" is Sirius's nickname, because of dogs' feet, and Sirius is the Dog Star.

Quidditch could be played with rocket-powered broomsticks and rocket-powered balls, with a computer program telling the balls to do whatever.

Harry Potter brings parents and children together, and many children who didn't read much before are reading *Harry Potter* now.

My mum, my brother, and I squabbled about who should read the fourth book first. Now I've started it. I was a bit worried about it, because it said in the papers that J. K. Rowling's plot had broken down! But she managed to reach the ending okay. I'm so glad.

∗

Andrea, *Goddard, Kansas*

I was in a bookstore, looking for a book to read on the way to Ireland. I just looked down, and there on the bottom shelf was the first Harry Potter book. I read the back cover and said, "This is the kind of book I've wanted to read my whole life." I have always known that I could write that kind of book, about magic and adventures.

The book interested me so much that everywhere we went on our trip—to Ireland, to see Big Ben [in London], and on the subways—I was reading the whole time. Nobody could stop me from finishing that book.

I love *Harry Potter* so much that I can't even express my feelings about it.

∗

Tonya, *Chandler, Arizona, 13 years old*

I have a couple of questions after reading the first three Harry Potter books thoroughly.

I still do not understand:

1. Why do parents want Harry Potter books banned from school?
2. Where did Dumbledore get that scar that matches the London Underground?
3. Is it true that all seven Harry Potter books have already come out in England?

◆▸ *Notes*

1. *Some parents think that children should not be encouraged to read the Harry Potter books because they believe that magic is evil. Their belief is based on their feelings or, in some cases, on the teachings of their spiritual leaders.*

    Two of the things that we learn from the Harry Potter books are that everyone should stand up for what he or she believes and that everyone is entitled to his or her opinion. These principles apply to those of us who believe the books are wholesome and educational, as well as to those who don't!

2. *Dumbledore's scar, which resembles a map of the London subway system, would come in handy if he ever got lost in London. Readers are left to guess whether he got the scar from a fight with another wizard, from a childhood fall, or from some other cause. Perhaps we will learn more about it in future J. K. Rowling books.*

3. *As of July 2000, Ms. Rowling had only published four Harry Potter books in the United Kingdom as well as in the United States.*

∗

Ariel and Ariana, *Weston, Florida*

Dear other Harry Potter fans,

We are very curious. We would be glad to share our questions and ideas. What would happen if a Muggle picked up a wand and happened to say "*Serpentia*" or "*Expelliarmus*"?

∗

Zoe, *Plymouth, Devon, England, 10 years old*

I really enjoy the Harry Potter books. I always read *Harry Potter* when I'm upset; somehow it makes me feel all bubbly and high in the sky!

My teacher, Mrs. Ward, also loves Harry Potter. I think if she has a baby boy she'll call it Harry.

∗

Alexis, *Landing, New Jersey, 9 years old*

I like the Harry Potter books because sometimes at recess I feel lonely, and there's always the Harry Potter books if I do.

∗

Steve, Jordan, and Brett,
Aurora, Colorado, 10, 8, and 5 years old

From Steve: My favorite kind of Every Flavor Beans would be barbecued ribs.

From Jordan: I would love to be a wizard. I like when the pictures move.

From Brett: I want to do spells so if someone is after me, I can put them to sleep. Then I could make a light saber by magic.

⋆

Carmelle, *Windsor, Ontario, Canada, 9 years old*

I've read the first two books and they are the best books in the world! I was shaking in my bed at the end of both of them!

Beverly Cleary used to be my favorite author, but now J. K. Rowling is! I want to be an author when I grow up, and I really want to be like her!

⋆

Melissa, *Grand Rapids, Michigan, 9 years old*

I wish I was a witch, and I wish I could go to Hogwarts (sigh). Oh, well, I do play witches with a friend, though.

I'd like to know when Harry Potter's birthday is and if he reads his own books.

I read the book *We Love Harry Potter,* and some of the kids and I think Harry should turn Dudley into a pig.

➥ *Note: We learn the date of Harry Potter's birthday on pages 141–142 of* Harry Potter and the Sorcerer's Stone.

⋆

Carla, *Kensington, Maryland, 11 years old*

What is most interesting about the Harry Potter books is that you have to not just read but to understand. You have to read between the lines. If you do this you will learn more about Harry and his world.

I think the Harry Potter books are so popular because everyone expects witches and wizards to soar on brooms and brew potions, but no one expects them to go to school, belong to different school houses, play Quidditch, or visit Diagon Alley.

One reason why everyone enjoys reading the books is all the different characters. Some are different (crazy), some are nice, mean, funny, smart (Hermione), ditsy, and brave.

I don't understand why some parents will not allow their kids to read *Harry Potter*, because it inspires witchcraft. Witchcraft is not real, so how can it be inspired? To really understand *Harry Potter*, you need to be somewhat intelligent, and you need to know that a kid can't jump out a window and fly. If kids don't know this, it's the fault of their parents, not J. K. Rowling.

✶

Arthur, *Tracy, California, 13 years old*

Lots of books I read are boring. I thought the Harry Potter books would be boring, too. I was wrong. I liked the last Harry Potter book I read because it was long. I also like it because you have to use your imagination. Once Albert Einstein said, "Imagination is more important than knowledge."

✶

Katherine, *St. Louis, Missouri*

When I read the Harry Potter books I truly feel I am in another world, a world of magic, wonder, excitement, and even danger. That world that I am in is real. I can leave all my other worries behind me. Few books can take me into such worlds as *Harry Potter* does.

At first, I was embarrassed being a teenager who enjoys "children's books." I have read each book several times, and once I start one of them, it becomes impossible for me to put it down. The suspense and mystery kill me, and I just have to read on. Some people say it's a shame to like such "children's fantasies," but I think the real shame and crime is *not* to like them.

✶

Victoria, *Bracknell, Berkshire, England, 13 years old*

All four Harry Potter books are brilliant. The way they are written is enchanting and realistic. Although they are made up, it is quite easy to believe them, especially when you are young. But adults too enjoy reading them to their children and they thoroughly enjoy them themselves!

J. K. Rowling writes books like I have never read before. The twists and turns and never-ending adventures make the books fun to read and hard to put down. I think the characters should stay the way they are.

∗

Stephanie, *Sussex, Wisconsin*

The reason that I and so many others like the Harry Potter books is because they take you away to a world that is filled with fun and suspense and so unlike ours. The books have a variety of genres, such as humor, suspense, scariness, and a happy ending that leaves you wanting to read the book that follows. There are characters who are lovable, hate-able, or just make you laugh. I don't like any character specifically because without one of them the story just wouldn't be complete. Such as Percy; many people want him gone, but I think that without Percy there would be no one for the twins to make fun of. Or without Percy there would be no one to dislike, which would make the stories too happy.

When you read the books it's as if you're actually there. You get a clear picture in your mind of how Hogwarts and its corridors look. But I think that the only person who knows truly what everything looks like is the person who is reading the book, because everyone has his or her own point of view about how things are in the books.

∗

Amanda, *Dos Palos, California, 13 years old*

I really wish I could go to Hogwarts to learn to be a witch. But then again, I don't. The Bible tells us that God does not want us to use sorcery, witchcraft, divination, or anything that involves magic. God wants us to trust the fact that he will take care of us.

But still, I wish we could use magic, just for fun! I do believe in magic, but I choose not to use it.

> ⟿ *Note: The wizard magic in J. K. Rowling's books is like our school subjects, such as mathematics, languages, or chemistry, which help us to expand our minds and understand our universe. Such understanding is very powerful in the real world, just as wizard magic is in Harry Potter's world.*

✱

Meredith, *Sydney, Australia, 11 years old*

After reading *We Love Harry Potter!*, I see how many people all over the world love it. Nearly all my class loves it.

I love how Hagrid tries to raise the dragon. I wish there was a Hogwarts school in Sydney.

✱

Lauren, *Follansbee, West Virginia*

When I read a Harry Potter book I feel like I'm inside the book, and I can't put it down. I loved the part in the third book about the Marauder's Map. The food sounds great. Butterbeer and Treacle Fudge were my favorites.

I would like to ask Hermione what it's like to be able to turn back time. I hope to see more of the Time-Turner in future books. I'm glad Hermione is really smart, because if she wasn't then the puzzles in the stories couldn't be solved.

✱

Jennifer, *Stonewall, Manitoba, Canada, 10 years old*

I couldn't help noticing a couple of mistakes in the book, *We Love Harry Potter!* In the back of the book, it says, "Some of us think that Harry's parents weren't exactly killed." This can't be true because in the fourth book, we learn information confirming

that they are, indeed, dead. Now don't get me wrong; I wish as much as the next person that Harry's parents were still alive, but I don't see any use in pretending that they are when they're not.

Also in the back of the book, it says, "After Harry's parents put a spell on him . . ." This is not correct. Harry's parents did not put a spell on him. Harry didn't die when Voldemort attacked him because his mother died to save him. I strongly suggest that you read Harry's fourth book to find some facts you missed.

>> *Note: Jennifer is perfectly correct about what we learn in the fourth book. However, if Jennifer had applied her detective talents just a little further, she might have noticed that* We Love Harry Potter! *was published in December 1999. (The publication date of a book appears on the second or fourth page.) Therefore, none of the children who contributed to that book had yet been able to read* Harry Potter and the Goblet of Fire, *which was published in July 2000.*

✳

Justine, *Whitefield, Manchester, England*

In *We Love Harry Potter!* you only really showed how the younger children like *Harry Potter*. I am in year 8 at school (second year, senior school) and still love *Harry Potter*. I plan to read all the others when they come out, even if I am in college! The feeling I get when I read the books is as if I am in the book, part of the story. It is a wonderful feeling.

I am an avid reader, just like my mum. When I started reading the books last year, my mum was constantly going on at me about how I should be reading classics, so I gave her a copy to read. She thought that it was brilliant, too! So brilliant that she bought me all the books.

I think that bringing out the new covers* for the Harry Potter books so that parents can also read them is stupid. Adults should not be ashamed to read children's books.

✳

Kevin, *Kamloops, British Columbia, Canada, 11 years old*

The Harry Potter books are the best ones I have ever read. I just can't stop reading them when it's time for bed. When I was

---

*There has been talk of issuing the Harry Potter books with plain covers in so-called "adult versions."

reading *Harry Potter and the Prisoner of Azkaban,* I hated to read the last chapter because there wasn't going to be any more to read!

∗

Andrew, *Medford, New Jersey*

My most favorite thing is the Every Flavor Beans. They are cool because it would be like having a bag of jelly beans that are really a bunch of computer chips or papers or tree branches or even blood! Whenever Quidditch is mentioned in the books I always get into it, for some reason. I love playing sports, but I don't think Quidditch is really a sport in the wizard world. It is a one-of-a-kind game that everyone just has to play to try to become the person with the most skills.

I wish that in our world we could have our own owls, and almost every day you would see them flying around with letters and maybe a package. Having magic in our world would mean we could become friends of Harry, Hermione, and Ron.

∗

Katherine, *Stroud, Gloucestershire, England, 15 years old*

The passion that comes through in the Harry Potter books and the emotion, are just unmeasurable. They have me in fits of giggles one minute and floods of tears the next.

When I first heard of Harry, I thought the books might be too young, but, as they say, never judge a book by its cover. It took me six hours to read the first one.

Harry finds his way into your heart. He becomes a friend. He is smart, brave, yet innocently young. He will never die, but live on as people keep reading the books. I have invested in my own copies so that when I leave home, they are going with me. If I ever have children, I want them to experience the magical world of Harry Potter.

J. K. Rowling has captured the hearts of the nation and even abroad! Her books have shown thousands the joy of reading.

∗

Rebekah, *Bucyrus, Ohio, 13½ years old*

I really, really love the Harry Potter books. My little brother and I have read all four of them. I love the way that Rowling puts things in the beginning of the book that seem unimportant, then at the end of the book you realize that it was actually very important.

I love the way Rowling makes everything seem so real. It's wonderful that she gives Harry problems and dilemmas like those every child goes through.

If anyone has a negative attitude about these books, he or she is ignorant of the fact that kids are actually reading more as a result of them. For example, almost everyone in my class of twenty-one has read the books. We even did a play based on them. They have also inspired many in my class to write, and not just little paragraphs or an extra letter to Aunt Betty, either, but books as long as 246 pages or twenty-five chapters. My teachers see nothing wrong with the fact that because kids are reading due to these books, their writing skills are advancing and their vocabularies and imaginations are soaring to new heights.

∗

Elaine, *Sydney, Australia, 11 years old*

Out of every single book I've ever read, the Harry Potter books are the best of them all! I don't know what I would have done without them. Ever day I try to picture what the next book will be about, what it will look like.

I like the first book because it starts to lead everything off, and the story begins, and the author unveils all her clever ideas like the funny words, Hogwarts, and of course, Harry!

I enjoyed the second book because the plot and the story line are the best I've ever seen.

The third book is full of surprises, and I think that it proves that things aren't always what they seem to be. The third book is my favorite.

If I had created a book, I would have created it exactly the same as J. K. Rowling did.

⋆

Mark, *Sprotbrough, Doncaster, England, 13 years old*

I would like to congratulate J. K. Rowling on the success and, more important, the quality of her books. The twists are always unexpected, the workings of the exciting parts are ingenious, and the details of the "world" are equal to that of Terry Pratchett's Discworld. I say that a good comic fantasy author adds a touch of magic to our world, but a great one adds a touch of our world to a magic one. I have read each of the Harry Potter books twice and intend to read them many times more. It is good that the author is unafraid to sacrifice some characters.

I am hoping to become an author myself and have started a book.

⋆

Dane, *Birmingham, Michigan*

How could I get an owl? Also, I would like a copy of a spell that makes lizards turn different colors.

⋆

Alicja, *Ontario, Canada, 8 years old*

I think Harry Potter books are good for children of all ages. I'm trying to learn how to be a wizard! It's hard work. In the first book, I like the part where Harry is in the maze and they had to solve all the puzzles.

★

Samuel, *Rome, Georgia*

If you don't like Harry Potter, I've got a lot of reasons why you should. Harry goes on adventures and does things we can't do, but maybe one day we can do those things.

★

Matilda, *London, England*

I am an English schoolgirl. I am from London and I live near J. K. Rowling. I wish I was Hermione and I always imagine I am her. The reasons I like *Harry Potter* are, one, it's a very long book, and two, you never know what's going to happen, do you?

➤ *Note: Matilda certainly lives nearer than we Americans do to J. K. Rowling, who lives in Edinburgh, Scotland.*

★

Ashleigh, *Anaheim, California, 13 years old*

I have read every book J. K. Rowling has made so far. I don't have a favorite book because every one is my favorite.

I think that these are more teenager/adult books, because there are puzzles to solve, and the vocabulary is up there in middle and high school. Also, my dad has read the first three and he loves them. He has recommended Harry Potter books to his friends to read.

Before I read the Harry Potter books I really disliked reading. My parents used to tell me to read, and I would make a big fuss about it. But now when my parents tell me to read, there is no problem, but now they don't even need to tell me to read. Every night I am caught up late reading *Harry Potter*, and I don't get to sleep until about 12 o'clock.

∗

Ginger, *Moweaqua, Illinois*

A friend and I have a question. Is it true that there was a Larry Potter? We heard there was a big controversy about him that post-poned the publishing of the fourth Harry Potter book. My friend and I were the ones who started reading the books at school. Now almost everyone at school has read them. I hope I can find out more about the big controversy.

➥ *Note: The controversy about "Larry Potter" was not a big one, and did not delay the publication of the fourth Harry Potter book.*

∗

Lauren and Sorcha, *London, England*

We're writing to discuss your book, *We Love Harry Potter!* We ap-preciate your writing a book for all the Harry Potter fans out there. However, we are not so pleased about your comments about where the story is based.

Harry makes it perfectly clear he loves the food at Hogwarts, yet a few of your letters suggest that if he were to live in America he wouldn't have to eat the terrible English food.

One of the letters even said that if Harry went to live in Amer-ica he would get to see better magical creatures than in England. I found this quite insulting towards England.

Also, in the chapter about Harry's parents, we didn't really un-derstand why you were trying to guess what magic Lily and James lived under, when the third book tells us. You might have started your book before the third book came out, but that is very unlikely.

We are certainly disappointed. After all, we were expecting a nice read but in the end we were quite offended.

➥ *Note: Of the seventy children who contributed to* We Love Harry Potter! *only three said they did not like the food. One was a vegetar-ian, who doesn't like to eat meat. Only one of these mentioned the fact that the food was English, and only one child suggested that there might be more magical animals in the United States because our country is larger and has more woods.*

A great many other children said in the book that they thought the Hogwarts food sounded very good.

One of the things we learn from the Harry Potter books is that everyone is entitled to his or her own opinion. A differing opinion is not the same as a deliberate insult. Sharing our opinions is a good way to learn more about the world.

Lauren and Sorcha are correct in assuming that the children who guessed about Harry's parents' magical past had not yet read the third book.

*

Erica, *Dyersville, Iowa, 11 years old*

I'm in the fifth grade. My teacher is Mrs. Wickham. She read the first book, *Harry Potter and the Sorcerer's Stone,* to us in class. It got me interested in the Harry Potter books.

The books really inspire me to read. I think kids are reading more because of the Harry Potter books.

*

Scott, *Gainsborough, Lincolnshire, England*

Most newspapers comment that J. K. Rowling has captured that "rare thing" in her books, but I think she's captured much, much more.

I have only one thought buzzing around in my head right now . . . will Dumbledore be able to stop Voldemort before it's too late?

*

Lana, *Sydney, Australia, 10½ years old*

I have thoroughly enjoyed the Harry Potter books. Today when I went to Dymock's booksellers I bought *The Diary of Harry*

Potter, and I asked the manager when the fourth Harry Potter book will be coming out. He said he wasn't sure, but when it does he'll definitely be reading it. So he must have read the first three books, too.

*

Meghan, *Wilmington, Ohio, 11 years old*

I really like the Harry Potter books, because of the suspense and thrill. I find it rather shocking that students spend seven years at Hogwarts and no one ever gets a bit homesick.

Some parts I don't understand. Like, why is it that the first year is the only year they sang the school song?

I think it would be difficult to get on a Quidditch team, so they should have other physical fitness activities for people who aren't on a Quidditch team.

➡ *Note: With each new Harry Potter book, we learn answers to questions that have puzzled us. That's one of the reasons we keep on reading the books!*

*

Kristine, *St. Croix, Nova Scotia, Canada*

I think the Harry Potter books are not only good to read, but good for your brain as well. They give half the story to your brain to imagine the rest.

*

Sabeena, *Auckland, New Zealand, 10 years old*

I have really enjoyed reading all the Harry Potter books. They are my very favorite books in the world.

Something that really surprised me was that my birthday is actually the same as Harry Potter's. But Harry is bigger than me!

★

Ann-Kathrin, *Birkenfeld, Germany, 13 years old*

I read Harry's adventures again and again. I think it's funny, interesting, and exciting to read about normal people who suddenly can do fantastic things. When I read the books, I think I'm in another world full of magic and wizards.

★

Caitlin, *Omaha, Nebraska*

When my mom first got me the first book in the Harry Potter series I thought it would be boring. Surprise! It wasn't! At first Hagrid scared me, but he turned into this really nice giant. It wasn't like the magic tales in which all the giants are mean and nasty.

Harry, Ron, Hermione, and Hagrid—I love them all! In *We Love Harry Potter!* all the kids wrote about their favorite parts. But to me, the characters are the most important!

★

Ted, *Visalia, California, 11 years old*

I don't read much, but when I pick up a Harry Potter book my imagination really comes alive. I think the books are a little boring at the beginning. Then, when Harry goes off to school, they get exciting.

I think that if I read the Harry Potter books I'll be a better reader, and I can write more creatively.

In future books, I think that Harry's parents should come back as ghosts.

★

Aidan, *Pontypool, Wales, 8 years old*

I really loved *Harry Potter and the Goblet of Fire*! I can't believe Vol . . . sorry, You-Know-Who has returned! It was really scary when Wormtail put that ugly snake-baby thing in the cauldron. But of course that made it more exciting. So, I would like to ask J. K. Rowling to please, please write the fifth book, or I'll turn myself into a frog or a toad.

★

Amanda, *Hoyleton, Illinois, 11 years old*

I savored everything about the astonishing Harry Potter books. I enjoy reading a lot, and I've never read a superior series. I think it is interesting how Harry lives with Muggles, who think he's nothing, but he really is famous.

I'd adore to go to wizard school and play Quidditch. I've figured out how to play Quidditch. I would be a Seeker.

My favorite animals are the owls and hippogriffs. They are kind and very helpful.

★

Hannah, *Parklands, Northampton, England, 9 years old*

Fantasy and adventures are my favorite kind of reading, so you can probably tell I enjoy reading *Harry Potter*. I think the ideas are very creative, especially the names of the characters.

I like the sound of Every Flavor Beans, but I would hate to get a toilet-water-flavored* one, though.

Why is Quidditch called Quidditch?**

I would find it hard to play Quidditch, as it is rather a complicated game. I would probably get the balls and the goals mixed up so I would score for the opposite team (if I ever did score, that is).

---

*Toilet water is another name for cologne.

**J. K. Rowling invented the name "Quidditch," probably by combining the names she gave to the three kinds of balls used in the game: the Quaffle, the Bludgers, and the Golden Snitch.

*

Allie, *Ulster, Pennsylvania*

I wonder how many books about Harry Potter J. K. Rowling is going to write? Maybe after she is done writing *Harry Potter* she should write mystery books.

> ➡ *Note: Ms. Rowling has said she plans to write seven Harry Potter books, one for each year Harry spends at Hogwarts. Many children, and adults, hope that she will write even more.*

*

Michael, *Princeton, Minnesota*

I am pretending I am a wizard and I would like to ask Dumbledore for some ideas. This is what I want to know: What are the ingredients for a sleeping potion? I want a map of wizard land. I need a map of Hogwarts, too.

*

Carleen, *Van Cleave, Mississippi*

I finished the fourth Harry Potter book last summer and can't wait for the fifth book. I love the way J. K. Rowling uses foreshadowing in her books. It gives a big clue about who's going to die later on in her books. I think it's Professor Snape whose death is foretold in the fourth book, on page 651, last paragraph.

I never thought many people liked the books until the fourth book came out and almost every bookstore had midnight parties. I watched them on the news.

*

Karen, *Dublin, Ireland*

I have blond hair, blue eyes, and I love reading J. K. Rowling's books. I can't wait till the next one comes out. My dad buys them for me. He reads them, too, only he reads them in two days. He's quicker than me, although I'm not that slow at reading. I can read one of the books in a week if I read it every day. The fact that the new book was bigger made it even more enjoyable.

Reading these books makes me wish things were really like that, and my dreams are even more exciting now, so I hope J. K. Rowling keeps writing.

∗

Drew, *Woodbury, Minnesota, 12 years old*

At first I disliked reading. Then my mom gave me *Harry Potter and the Sorcerer's Stone,* and I thought it was the most exciting book I have ever read!

A lot of kids at my school have read all the books and I need to catch up. I have started *Harry Potter and the Chamber of Secrets,* and I also love that book. If I were Uncle Vernon, I would not lock Harry up because anything can happen (wink, wink).

∗

Jason, *Orton Brimbles, Peterborough, England, 10 years old*

Harry Potter is brilliant! I love Quidditch, even though I've never played it. I once had a dream that I was in Hogwarts and I was playing Quidditch. When I woke up I was really disappointed that it was a dream.

No other book has made me keep reading as long as *Harry Potter,* and that's really saying something, because if I don't like a book I put it down.

∗

Alexa, *East Amherst, New York, 8 years old*

J. K. Rowling is probably the most creative person I've ever heard of or read about. Her stories are so good that we just have to keep our eyes glued to the book. She is my inspiration because she is the most amazing person!

Hagrid is one of my favorite characters because there would be no *Harry Potter* without him!

*

Kirsty, *Chelmsley Wood, Birmingham, England, 12 years old*

At the turn of the century, I didn't even know who Harry Potter was, let along his wonderful schooling at Hogwarts. I heard about Harry's adventures at school, when one boy based his leaflet [school report] upon Harry Potter.

I read the first book after discovering the paperback in my school library. I was hypnotized, and after a week I took out the second book. Then along came the third, which I borrowed off a friend. Then I bought the fourth book, which is my most favorite book as it was a lot longer than the other three and I got to enjoy the ways of Hogwarts for over three hundred more pages.

I would like to thank Ms. Rowling for changing my life forever. She has brought on a new era of enjoyable fantasy books for children across the world.

*

Owen, *Victoria, Australia, 10 years old*

My mum and dad like the Harry Potter books, too. I am skinny, about 4'10" with brown hair. My friend Timothy says I look like Harry because I have a scar on my forehead from having a swing hit me accidentally. Besides J. K. Rowling, my favorite authors are C. Day Lewis, Roald Dahl, Enid Blyton, and Duncan Ball.

*

Lindsay, *De Kalb, Illinois, 17 years old*

What I like about the Harry Potter books is that they have a plot, very detailed, and you can tell what the characters might look like by using your imagination.

My grandma Ann had the first and third books for herself and for me. She said they were really good. Soon I had read all four books and became a Harry Potter freak!

Then I got two good books about J. K. Rowling and Harry Potter, *We Love Harry Potter!* by Sharon Moore, and *An Unauthorized Biography of J. K. Rowling* by Marc Shapiro. The biography book tells about her life and how she came up with the idea about the books.

I'm a senior in high school. My goal in life is to be a herpetologist (a person who studies reptiles and amphibians). My favorite animal is the alligator.

★

A family from Lakewood, Ohio:

Miriam (Mitzi), *12 years old;*
Sarai, *4 years old;*
Yosef and Rivka, *8 years old; and*
Chana and Chaya, *10 years old*

Mitzi: We are all Harry Potter fans. Each of my sisters and my brother has each written down something about the Harry Potter books. Since I am the oldest and have the neatest handwriting, everyone dictated his or her comments to me.

My friend Helen Patrice (initials are a coincidence) says it doesn't make sense for Hogwarts to celebrate Christmas, if it isn't a Christian school. She also says Harry can't have a godfather, since he wasn't baptized.

Sarai: I think Neville is the funniest of all the *Harry Potter* characters. I did not understand why Professor McGonagall was so furious with him for writing down a week's worth of passwords. I always do things like that.

Yosef: I am sorry Sirius Black played that trick on Professor Snape and he ended up indebted to the Potters. I didn't think it was one bit funny, and I would have hated Mr. Lupin, Mr. Potter, and Mr. Black forever. I understand why they don't like Harry Potter.

Rivka: I understand why Dudley bullied Harry. I treat my sister

Sarai the same way and I give her dumb presents. I think if I was living with Harry Potter, the way Dudley does, I would want to kill him.

Chana: I would hate to be in the Harry Potter stories. For one thing, I'm a Jew, and all the holidays Hogwarts ever celebrates are Christian. No Kwanzaa, Ramadan, Chanukah, or Purim. For another thing, I wouldn't like to have magic powers I'm not allowed to use. And also, I like being normal, outside and inside.

Chaya: I thought the Quidditch chapter in the *We Love Harry Potter!* book was exceedingly unhelpful. The recipe chapter was pretty good, though.

*

Claire, *Plymouth, Devon, England*

I go to boarding school in Somerset and am in the senior year there, so I rarely have time to read, which is a hobby. So when I first started to read *Harry Potter*, I couldn't put the book down. Even some of the teachers said I was quieter than usual. I read every spare moment I had, but when I got to a really good part and then went to lessons, I usually read during the lesson and then got detention for not listening!

I read the first two books in a week because I usually read after lights-out. Then I read the third one over the weekend. I recently read them again because I didn't have anything else to read. I really enjoyed reading *Harry Potter* and can't wait until more are published.

*

Jennifer, *Vernon, British Columbia, Canada, 9 years old*

I can't wait for the next book [the fourth one]. It will be so fun. I hear it has the scariest ending of all the books so far.

I don't think there should be movies for any of the books. They're good the way they are right now. The books are more interesting than a movie about them would be.

∗

Stephanie, *Leamington Spa, Warwickshire, England, 9 years old*

I really like the Harry Potter books. The third book is very funny, especially when the fortune-telling teacher said, "No, do not ask me, I will not say another word" or something like that.

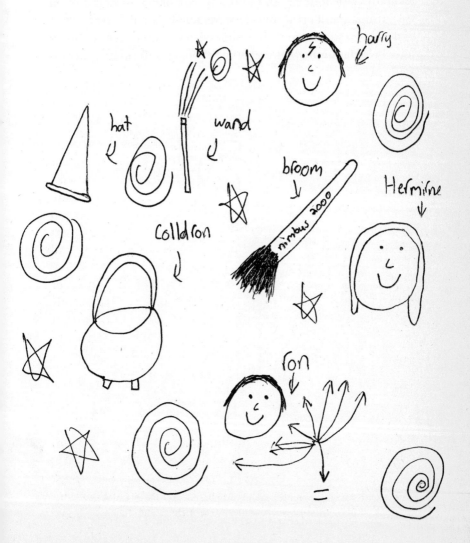

★

Grace, *Charleroi, Victoria, Australia, 10 years old*

My favorite Harry Potter book so far is the first book because it didn't freak me out. My sister Elle and I love the books. I wish I were Harry. I work like Hermione, though; I do like doing lots of [school] work at home, so I'm the best at all my subjects. I'm the best at math and art in my class. My family is very artistic. Mum makes pots, which we're not allowed near, so we often have to have breakfast, lunch, or tea* somewhere away from her pots.

*Tea is sometimes the evening meal in Australia, comparable to Americans' supper and unlike British tea, which is a light meal taken in the late afternoon.

Our Most and Least Favorite Characters:

The Good Guys and the Bad Guys

In the Harry Potter books, there are characters we love and characters we love to hate. Even the villains are exciting! Here are some children's feelings about the major characters.

*

Jacqueline, *Canyon Country, California, 10 years old*

I like Hermione. She's smart, but she needs a life. She is too involved with books, and she's a bit of a tattletale.

Madam Trelawny freaks me out.

I like Cho Chang. She is Asian, just like me. I hope I see her again in other Harry Potter books.

I'm glad Mrs. Norris got petrified. I love cats, except for Mrs. Norris. She's annoying, but Crookshanks was nice.

If I played Quidditch, I'd want to be a Seeker and have a Firebolt and knock the Slytherins off their brooms. I'd especially aim for Malfoy to teach him a lesson.

⋆

Kathleen, *Totten, Southampton, England, 11 years old*

I greatly admire Ms. Rowling's books. They give me an inspiration to be an author when I'm older, and hopefully I'll be as successful as she is.

Sometimes my dad moans at me for reading the books instead of paying attention to him!

If I were Harry, I would turn Dudley into a nice big fat pig! I doubt if you'd be able to tell the difference, though. Hermione must be a real pain. I can see why Harry likes her, but can't she have any fun? I must admit I admire her brain. Ron's cool, but of all people I didn't expect him to have a phobia about spiders!

⋆

Whitney, *Papillion, Nebraska, 11 years old*

If Harry had been a girl, Lily and James would have named her Harriet, and instead of being fearless and brave she would have been shy and thoughtful. Harriet would have been able to think things through and wouldn't have broken as many rules. Oliver Wood would have been even more curious, if Harry was Harriet. She probably still would have saved the day and lived up to her name, but she probably also would have written thank-you cards to people who deserved them (like those who gave Harry candy when he was in the hospital wing at the end of the first book).

Of course, who really wants to know what it would be like if Ron was Ronnie and Hermione was Herman? Imagine that! Things would have been hectic!

⋆

Megan, *Barrie, Ontario, Canada, 14 years old*

When I picked up the first book and started reading it, I got sucked right into Harry's world. I really wonder where J. K. Rowling gets all the names for things, like "Hogwarts," "Muggle," and

"Dumbledore." It would be great to have friends like Ron and Hermione. You can trust them and you always have fun when they're around.

I feel really bad for Harry because he has to live with the Durs-leys. He can't talk to them about things.

The fourth book is my favorite, and by far the scariest. I can't wait for the next one to come out. I really want to see what happens with Voldemort now that he is risen.

> ●→ *Note: The name J. K. Rowling gave to Harry's school is probably a pun based on syllables used in English place names (such as "ham" and "wich") and on "warthog," which is a kind of wild pig. "Muggle" may be another of her puns, based on "mug," or low-class person, and the ordinary human's tendency to "bungle" or "muddle" things. "Dumbledore" is an Old French word for "bumblebee." One of J. K. Rowling's creative gifts is her ability to combine words she has learned, perhaps through her own reading, and use them to form descriptive and amusing names for places and people.*

*

Tim, *Blair, Nebraska, 10 years old*

Harry Potter isn't what you would call a great student, and he doesn't really follow the rules.

Quidditch is probably the most dangerous sport. And one game could last a couple of months!

Dumbledore is a little bit mad, but he's a genius and amazing.

I'm going to a Harry Potter party at a bookstore, and everyone gets to buy the new book a second after midnight.

*

Stephanie, *Lombard, Illinois, 9 years old*

Hermione is one of my favorite people in the Harry Potter books. It would be funny if she got hit with a spell that made her dumb! And Malfoy would get expelled because he shot it at her. In the future books I hope there are more people like Hermione.

∗

Ben, *Norwich, Norfolk, England*

I wish I could get a picture of Mr. and Mrs. Dursley, because all my friends have different ideas about what they look like.

∗

Monique, *Saugus, Massachusetts, 11 years old*

When I read the Harry Potter books they make me feel like I'm really there.

I heard that Whoopi Goldberg is going to be in the Harry Potter movie. I think she should be Professor McGonagall.

∗

Rabea, *Hamtramck, Michigan, 11 years old*

My favorite character is Harry, because he is so brave and tries to save Hogwarts from harm.

I believe that Harry's parents are still alive. I hope Harry breaks the spell that's been put on them and finds them, or meets them somehow as Animagi.

∗

Deborah, *Singapore, 11 years old*

I have read all four Harry Potter books, and I find them easy to understand but amazing.

My favorite characters are Harry, Ron, Hermione, Cho Chang, Fred, and George. Fred and George made me laugh about the Ton-Tongue Toffee they gave to Dudley.

I hate Malfoy, Snape (he was unfair and I shan't call that git a professor), Crabbe, Goyle, and the Dursleys. I also hate Rita Skeeter, as her Quick-Quotes Quill writes lies.

I would take all of the subjects, yes, even Potions—except Muggle Studies and Divination (they are boring)—to ensure that I am a smart witch, yet not so much that I go berserk.

In the final book, I want Voldemort to die. And in the next book, I hope Sirius is able to take Harry to live in his house.

∗

Caroline, *Old Wethersfield, Connecticut, 11 years old*

I have no idea why I like the Harry Potter books so much. It seems like it's on the tip of my tongue, but I just can't put my finger on it.

There are two words for why I like Hermione: girl power! She's witty, smart, yet a good friend.

The Dursleys should be called the Dudleys because Dudley gets all the attention. I think if I were Harry I'd go dig a hole and plant Aunt Petunia in it. Dudley should go three birthdays and Christmases without presents, and Mr. Dursley should spend a few days behind bars.

Since I don't like sports that much, I'd probably stink at Quidditch, but I'd try anyway. I'd like to see a new girl come to school, and I think Harry Potter should have a crush on her.

∗

Caron, *Seneca, South Carolina*

Ever since I read the first Harry Potter book, I've always wished there was a way that I could live in the wizarding world. I'd give anything to be able to attend Hogwarts, visit Hogsmeade and Diagon Alley, and ride on the Hogwarts Express.

I don't know about anybody else, but I'd like to have either Hedwig or "Pig" as a pet.

I love every character in the books, except for Snape, Voldemort, and Malfoy and his gang.

I love Quidditch. It's a neat and creative sport. Especially the Seeker's job; it's the most thrilling part of the game.

*

Ashlee, *Picnic Point, Australia, 13 years old*

I think Harry should turn the Dursleys into animals—Vernon and Dudley into pigs and Petunia into an emu. I think Harry is kinda cute. If he's ever looking for a girlfriend, he should send me an owl.

I think Hermione is a bit too much of a goody-goody. So I have some pointers for her:

• Don't suck up to teachers all the time.

• Read novels instead of textbooks!

I think it's cool that Hagrid has all those amazing animals. I'm especially fond of Aragog because I love spiders. Most people think girls hate spiders; I don't. But I shudder to think that he might eat me.

*

Shalmai, *Lowell, Massachusetts, 12 years old*

I just got the fourth Harry Potter book yesterday, and I've already finished all 734 pages of it. I am curious about one thing in it. The maid found all three Riddles dead. Voldemort was still alive, though. Did he stage his own death?

It is very strange that every year the students have a new Defense Against the Dark Arts teacher. A lot of people are prejudiced against the creatures they don't totally understand, like werewolves and giants. They all can't be bad. I mean, they can't help being what they are.

� *Note: Shalmai raises an interesting question about the Riddles. J. K. Rowling no doubt planted this mystery for her readers to puzzle over and hopefully she will solve it in one of her future books.*

∗

Attila, *Calgary, Alberta, Canada, 9½ years old*

I absolutely, positively love the Harry Potter books. What I like about them is that you never know what happens next. I also enjoy the humor, like when Ron and Hermione are always bickering. It surprised me so much in the fourth book, when Ron and Harry stop being friends temporarily for the first time ever! Even though I was more on Harry's side, I did understand Ron for being a bit jealous of all the attention Harry gets.

If I had to choose a favorite, it would be the fourth. The idea of the Triwizard Tournament was fantastic! Ingenious really, how Harry and the other champions had to do the three tasks. The third book really gripped me. I was so worried that Harry might be killed! In the second book, I was so hooked. I just had to know who Riddle was! In the first book, I nearly died of surprise when I turned the page and read who it was who tried to kill Harry.

I roll my eyes at the very thought of Filch and Mrs. Norris.

I'd enjoy the food they eat at Hogwarts, because I do not like vegetables, but I do like meat and potatoes. I'd love to try butterbeer and Chocolate Frogs. In Hogsmeade, I'd for sure try to buy myself an Invisibility Cloak, and also Dr. Filibuster's Fabulous, Wet-Start, No-Heat Fireworks.

∗

Eunice, *Long Beach, California, 9 years old*

I felt very sorry for Harry when I heard that his parents died. If it wasn't for my friend Elyssa Schmidt I wouldn't even know that! I hope that in the next book Hermione stops acting like a brat or a big smarty-pants. I think that in the third book, when Harry and Hermione went back in time, they should have caught Scabbers. I think I know what Hagrid has. I think the pink umbrella isn't an umbrella—I think it's a wand. I wish I were a witch.

∗

Shenin, *Kittanning, Pennsylvania, 10 years old*

In the Harry Potter books, if Mrs. Norris is a Mrs., then what happened to *Mr.* Norris?

◆◆ *Note: Good question! We know that tomcats do not make good husbands, because they tend to wander off and not return. Perhaps that is what Mr. Norris did.*

∗

Kaval, *St. Mary's, Tasmania, Australia, 7 years old*

I have read all four Harry Potter books. I am an advanced reader.

I like all the characters except the Slytherins and Filch.

My favorite was Hermione. I look a lot like her. I also liked Pigwidgeon and Hedwig. Madam Pomfrey was all right.

I'd like an Invisibility Cloak, and I like the food. I liked when Voldemort appeared in the fourth book.

∗

Jasmin, *Paso Robles, California, 9 years old*

My favorite teachers in the third book were Hagrid and Trelawney. Professor Trelawney is neat because she can tell the future! I sure am glad her prediction about Harry was wrong at the end.

My favorite ghost is Nearly Headless Nick. I wonder if he can chop off the bit of his neck that's left and join the Headless Hunt?

My dad loves reading *Harry Potter* to my brother and me.

I love Quidditch. I would like to be a Seeker just like Harry.

✳

Briahna, *Jim Falls, Wisconsin, 11 years old*

My favorite book is the third one, and my favorite person is Professor Remus Lupin. I don't know why; maybe it's because I like wolves so much. I was very disappointed at the end of the book when he had to leave. I hope he comes back in another book; he even told Harry they'd meet again.

Why do people want a Harry Potter book about Quidditch so much? I mean, I like Quidditch, but a whole book on it?!

✳

Garrett, *Jacksonville, Florida, 8 years old*

I like the Harry Potter books. It's very strange, but hardly anyone in my class likes Harry.

I hate the clothes the Dursleys give to Harry.

I like Hedwig. She seems very peaceful.

➤ *Note: Garrett's mother recently wrote us that, since reading the Harry Potter books four times, Garrett has read thirty more books. She thinks that's why he won the third- and fourth-grade spelling bee (he's now nine and in the third grade).*

✳

Chela, *North Vancouver, British Columbia, Canada, 13 years old*

I think it's cool the way Hermione stands up for herself and her friends, like in the third book when she slapped Malfoy in the

face. I must say, I was not expecting that. I think Pansy Parkinson from Slytherin was jealous when Hermione went to the Yule Ball with Krum in the fourth book.

*

Stephen, *South Hadley, Massachusetts*

Hermione is so smart and responsible. She deserves to be a prefect and head girl when she is older. My favorite adventures were when she made the Polyjuice Potion in Moaning Myrtle's bathroom and when she and Harry went back with the Time-Turner. I especially liked it when she figured out the jar [bottle] problem in the end of the first book. I think she is the brains of the trio [Hermione, Harry, and Ron] and that she is a necessity at Hogwarts. If you think about it, where would the school be without her?

∗

Carle, *Livermore, California, 11 years old*

I wish I was a good witch and went to school with Harry. He is cute and a nice guy, even if he is older than me. Mr. Snape I think goes a little too far when he gets mad at Harry. Mr. Dumbledore is a cool principal. He is better than our principal, Mr. Young. I would love to go on Harry's new broom, the Firebolt, the fastest broom on Earth. No one should be as cruel as the Dursleys are to Harry, even if they have a purpose to swish the magic out of him.

∗

Maristela, *Silverdale, Washington, 8 years old*

I like how Harry Potter solves mysteries and puzzles. My favorite mystery was when Harry didn't know who sent him the Firebolt.

∗

Jessie, *Cape Cod, Massachusetts, 11 ½ years old*

I wish I were Harry's best girlfriend except for Hermione. I hope J. K. Rowling writes more than seven books so I can find out what Harry is like when he is out of school and who he marries, if he gets married.

I like all the Weasleys, especially the twins, Fred and George. I hate the Dursleys. Living with them like Harry does must be like a lifetime of cleaning your room.

∗

Joe, *Chagrin Falls, Ohio, 9 years old*

I like the Harry Potter books because I can imagine every character, except Professor Trelawney. My favorite animal is

Crookshanks because he is so intelligent. I like Ron because he's exciting and funny. I like Neville because he's forgetful and proud.

I don't know how Harry survived Voldemort three times. I'd like to live with Hagrid.

∗

Elizabeth, Erin, and Danielle, *Torrington, Connecticut*

Our favorite book so far is the fourth. Elizabeth likes Professor McGonagall because she exemplifies a good teacher, and because she is fair and honest. Danielle likes Hermione because she gives the girls who read the books someone to look up to. Erin likes Hagrid because he cares about Harry, Ron, and the other students.

∗

Miranda, *Belmont, Massachusetts, 10 years old*

I think Neville is one of the best and funniest characters in the books. He needs to work on magic a bit more. If he had used magic when he was fighting Crabbe and Goyle, he probably would have won. It would be cool to have a Remembrall, like Neville does. It would be helpful for me, since I forget a lot. I wish it would tell you *what* you forgot, though.

∗

Sarah, *Columbus, Indiana, 9 years old*

My favorite character in the books is Peeves. He was really funny. My favorite animal is Fluffy. I'd like a three-headed dog. Really, in a way, I do have a two-headed dog. I have three dogs, and two of them, Fritter and her daughter Snoozy, play together all the time and it looks like they are one dog!

My least favorite animal is Scabbers.

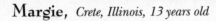

Margie, *Crete, Illinois, 13 years old*

Every kid in England and America should be glad that God put Jo Rowling on Earth, because she is the creator of Harry Potter. Harry has been an influence on many kids, especially me. I would like to grow up to become more like Harry, Ron, and Hermione. Harry because he is bold and brave, Ron because he is funny, and Hermione because she is smart and clever.

One of my dreams is for my name to be put in a Harry Potter book. I would like to be in Ravenclaw.

I'll bet Harry would love to transfigure Dudley into a warthog or something like that.

I'd like to ask Hermione if they have any music groups in the wizard world. I would love to be as smart as she is. I mean, how does she do it? I would like to ask her for any advice that might help me. I think she should ease up on Ron sometimes. He just wants to have fun!

I'm actually kind of happy that Ron got rid of Scabbers. He was just holding Ron down, anyway.

Cassandra, *Laredo, Texas, 10 years old*

I don't know how J. K. Rowling came up with the Harry Potter books. I can't believe someone could write such amazing books. They are my favorites, and, believe me, I've read a lot of books. My

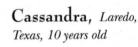

city is trying to banish the books because they involve magic and evil. I know that the books are fiction, so I don't care.

The plot in each book is completely different, and each plot is magical and each plot is complicated. So you have to be an understanding reader.

I have two favorite characters: Harry and Hermione. Harry is brave, smart, has a big heart, cares about others, and did I mention I love his eyes?

I also like Hermione because she is kind of pretty, very smart, and reminds me, well, of me.

*

Ashlyn, *Elizabeth, Pennsylvania, 10 years old*

Harry is so brave and famous but yet so humble. He isn't scared of much, is he? I never had a teacher pick on me, but it must be embarrassing. He is lucky to have Hermione as his friend, otherwise he might have drunk the wrong potion [in the first book] and died. We wouldn't want that to happen, would we?

I couldn't believe who was the Slytherin's heir.

I really admire Hagrid. I almost cried when I read that Buckbeak was going to be executed. I like how Hagrid takes care of all kinds of magical creatures like Buckbeak, Fluffy, Fang, and Norbert. I also like how Hagrid talks. The books would not be as interesting if Hagrid were not in them!

*

Grace, *San Francisco, California, 11 years old*

I would love to go to Hogwarts! I was so disappointed this summer when I didn't get an application form. I am so jealous of Cho Chang, so I kind of don't like her. Harry Potter, Ron, and Hermione are my favorite main kid characters. My other favorite kid characters are Parvati Patil and Padma Patil. I like Parvati Patil because she gets to dance with Harry in the fourth book.

I want to try to get into the movie and be Parvati Patil, but my mom and dad think that there's a small chance of it and I don't live in Britain but I so want to! And not because of money or fame, but because it's the closest I'll ever get to going to Hogwarts and meeting Harry, Ron, and Hermione.

∗

Kristina, *Northumberland, Pennsylvania, 13 years old*

I think Harry is a great person, brave, mischievous, and adventurous. Hermione is so smart, but she's starting to loosen up a bit. She puts a lot of pressure on herself. I really like Hagrid. I always feel bad for him when Draco Malfoy makes fun of him.

The Weasley twins and Lee Jordan are so funny, especially when Jordan is commentating at Quidditch matches.

The animals in the books are very interesting, but I agree with Ron that spiders are disgusting!

I would love to live at Hogwarts! And the food! No, I definitely wouldn't mind living at Hogwarts.

Since I absolutely love sports, I adore Quidditch. I'd love to play Seeker, but I'd settle for Chaser. I miss Oliver Wood as the Gryffindor Quidditch Captain. He sounds a lot like me.

I think J. K. Rowling must have a good imagination and a great sense of humor to write such books!

∗

Diana, *Merritt Island, Florida, 12 years old*

The Harry Potter books are really page-turners. My favorite character is Neville Longbottom because it seems like everyone is always teasing him. Besides, I'm accident-prone myself. I also like Oliver Wood, the Quidditch Captain for Gryffindor, because he gets so involved in the game. And because of that, the team almost always wins! If I could play Quidditch, I'd like to play Chaser.

My favorite book so far is *Harry Potter and the Prisoner of Azkaban* because of all the funny parts, especially where the Marauder's

Map starts to insult Snape! But what is an "ugly git"? I've been wondering about that.

➥ *Note: "Git" is a coarse British slang word for a low-born, good-for-nothing person.*

*

Siobhan, *Newton Abbot, Devon, England, 11 years old*

Lots of books are good, but not as good as *Harry Potter.*

I love Hedwig because she's so beautiful. I think Harry should get Cho to be his girlfriend because they are both excellent Seekers. The food is really weird. I'd love to try all the flavors of Bertie Bott's Every Flavor Beans. I really like Hagrid—even though he has a misleading approach he is really gentle. I'd love to play Quidditch, but on the ground it wouldn't work.

As for Ron, it must be really good to have five brothers and a sister, especially if your whole family are wizards.

*

Drew, *Columbus, Ohio, 10 years old*

I think Harry should say something to Hermione to get her to stop acting like she's a know-it-all.

*

Michelle, *Chatsworth, California, 9 years old*

I've read the first three Harry Potter books and can't wait for the rest! My aunt introduced them to me.

My favorite character is Hagrid because he's nice and brave. He can be a little overprotective of Harry at times. Malfoy, Crabbe, Goyle, Voldemort, and Snape are mean. They give you someone to hate, though! I hated it when Malfoy ruined Hagrid's first class. I wanted to cry, because Hagrid really wanted to be a

teacher. I'd like Every Flavor Beans and Chocolate Frogs. I'd hate to get a gross bean, though!

In my class, we're reading the first book. It's fun to know what's going to happen when everyone else doesn't!

*

Abbey, *Waunakee, Wisconsin, 11 years old*

My favorite character is Hermione. She has bushy brown hair and dark eyes just like me!

Sometimes I go to the local bookstore and sit and read anything and everything about Harry. I have entered just about every Harry Potter contest I heard of but I haven't won yet!

I feel bad for Harry because he has to stay with the Dursleys. I am also jealous of him because I would love to go to wizard school and play Quidditch.

✶

Katherine, *San Angelo, Texas, 13 years old*

I think Hermione is the most important person in the Harry Potter books, because in the first book, she helped Harry with his homework and through all the obstacles to get to the Sorcerer's Stone. So basically, if she hadn't been there, Harry would have either had to drop off the Quidditch team or fail all his classes. Plus, she's the only girl.

I am going to be sad when the seventh book comes out, because that is the last one. But if J. K. Rowling needs some helpful hints for some of her books, then I'll be glad to help.

My father, who's a big fan of the Harry Potter books, has this theory about Harry's parents. He thinks that his mother is somehow Hedwig and his father is Crookshanks. I'm not sure about it, but it would be really cool.

I think Harry and Ginny would make a sort of ironic couple, but Harry likes Cho so much. . . .

It would be really nice, if there is an extra page or two, to put a pronunciation list in one of the books!

✶

Angela, *Gonzales, California, 12 years old*

I like the Harry Potter books because the characters are excellent, the illustrations are grand, and they're wonderful books. You see, I am in seventh grade and I can read at college level. I'm what people call an advanced reader. These books aren't like any other books, because you can't put them down until you get to the ultimate climax.

Most of the books I read are boring at the end. The Harry Potter books always keep me at the edge of my seat. Literally, my mouth fell open when I found out who wanted to steal the Sorcerer's Stone. The names are hilariously funny.

The wizards on the cards in the Chocolate Frogs are compara-

ble with those in our history, like Merlin, the faithful wizard of King Arthur, and Circe, the witch who turned men into pigs.

I am a meat-and-potatoes girl, so I like the food in the books.

I have no idea why some people don't like the Harry Potter books. Like my sister-in-law. I love her and all, but she doesn't want me to read them. My mom likes me reading them but my sister-in-law doesn't. *Harry Potter* has to be the best book I have ever read.

I think Harry's friends are totally cool. I have a couple of friends like them. Their names are Kathleen, Aijay, Lizzie, and Marissa.

I wonder why Crabbe and Goyle stick up for Malfoy? He is smaller than they are and they could beat him up. Malfoy is a total jerk, dork, square, and Slytherin weenie.

*

Bailey, *Lebanon, Ohio, 11 years old*

My favorite part of the Harry Potter series was in the third book, when Harry was playing the Ravenclaw house for the school Quidditch Cup. And then he sees Cho Chang, the Ravenclaw seeker, and he thinks she's cute!

It's funny how Ron wishes that he was a star like Harry, but in the world that we live in he *is* a star, just as big as Harry is.

✳

Sarah, *Hammond, Indiana, 10 years old*

I hate how some people criticize Hermione. I think she's a brilliant character, and just because she told Professor McGonagall about Harry's Firebolt doesn't mean she's untrustworthy. It just shows how much she cares about Harry. If she hadn't told the teacher and the broom had been jinxed, then Harry might have been killed.

Some people also say that Lily Potter [Harry's mother] wasn't as good a wizard as James [Harry's father] because her family are all Muggles. This is not true. Look at Hermione. She is Muggle-born, and she is the best witch at Hogwarts.

✳

Sarah, *Ann Arbor, Michigan, 11 years old*

My favorite character in the Harry Potter books is Ron. He is so funny. I also like the Weasley twins. I have a friend named Chris who looks like the way Ron is described, but he has much lighter hair. I also know a friend who looks like Ginny would. I like Snape, too.

If Malfoy and his friends made fun of Ron or his family, I would punch him. I am probably bigger than them, anyway. I am five feet four or five inches tall.

✳

Michael, *Milan, Pennsylvania*

I think J. K. Rowling's books are super-good but I think she should add more friends for Harry. Ron is my second-favorite character, but the author should add more details about Ron. I think Ron needs to be a bit smarter.

Hermione is my least-favorite character because she likes to be so perfect. I don't like people that much who act like they're perfect. I still do like Hermione, but I wish J. K. Rowling would add more school friends for Harry.

★

Katie, *Cincinnati, Ohio, 11 years old*

When I finished reading all the Harry Potter books, I read the other books I had at home and really got bored. So I'm reading them all over again.

Harry, Hermione, and Ron are really great friends. They can agree on things. I don't know why, but I think there's something different about Neville.

I think Hagrid is really nice, but likes to keep his privacy. I believe Snape is good, but is really good at hiding it. Like my dad said, Malfoy is just plain stupid.

Quidditch sounds really cool. I've always dreamed of flying.

★

John, *East Williston, New York, 12 years old*

I think Hagrid is so cool. It must be great to be so tall! I'm tall for my age, too. I'm only twelve years old and I am five feet four inches tall. I wonder if Hagrid has ever been made fun of because of his height?

I would like to ask Hagrid if he has ever made his own food?

I think Hagrid should write a book called *Magical Creatures and Me.*

➥ *Note: In several of the Harry Potter books, Hagrid sometimes did his own cooking. He was a notoriously bad cook.*

✳

Monica, *Lakewood, Ohio*

I personally think that Harry (under the condition of the rudeness of the Dursleys) should be able to do magic at their house. I would love to see what he could do to Dudley!

Sneaking around unnoticed in an Invisibility Cloak would be fun. My favorite characters are Fred and George Weasley, because they are pranksters and they make me laugh.

My two really smart uncles, Uncle Will and Uncle Tom, are smart but not nearly as wise as Dumbledore. I would love to chat with him and get advice.

Collecting cards that come with Chocolate Frogs would be fun, especially since the characters move!

Hagrid is big, lovable, friendly, big, funny, and well, just plain big! Meeting Norbert would be an experience I would never forget. I wouldn't want to get too close, though!

★

Tara, *Shippenville, Pennsylvania, 8 years old*

I am sorry that Dobby was Mr. Malfoy's house-elf. It was probably torture! I would like Dobby to be my house-elf.

★

Erin, *Abilene, Texas, 11 years old*

I love to read, so I have lots of favorite books. My favorite types are fantasy, so the Harry Potter books are right up my alley.

I hope that Harry has a girlfriend in the future books, but I *do not* think it should be Cho Chang. I think it should be Ginny Weasley. Ginny is a sweet, sensitive, love-struck girl. I bet they would make the perfect couple. I would like to hear more about Ginny and Cho Chang, too.

I liked Hagrid a lot. Even though he was a giant, he was sensitive and kind. So it came as no surprise when I found out about his love for animals. No matter how ferocious, terrifying, hideous, or gruesome a creature was, he only saw the good in it.

I am mostly like Hermione Granger. I am smart, tend to overdo things, and am usually the leader in a crisis. I loved Crookshanks. I love how proud and haughty he is. He acts just like my cat, May.

I had a teacher like Professor Snape. Snape isn't really mean, he's just harsh. I think that he must have a reason for being the way he is.

★

V. Siddharth, *Chennai, Madras, India, 12 years old*

My name is Siddharth. I am an avid reader of Harry Potter books. I have read the first three Harry Potter books at least three times each. I like Harry, Ron, Dumbledore, Professor McGonagall, Professor Flitwick, and Hagrid. I don't like Hermione as much as Ron and Harry, because she is kind of bossy.

I notice one thing that has not been published in any of the books—what is Harry's favorite professional Quidditch team?

✳

Dylan, *Everett, Washington, 12 years old*

I would like the Harry Potter series to continue until Harry dies at an old age. The part I like best about the school is that there are no subjects like science, math, or physical education, because really there is no need for it. Harry, Ron, and Hermione are usually quite weird about the adventures that go on. Hermione is always wanting it done to her complete satisfaction, Harry is always patient and concerned, and Ron is just ready to go for it. He seems like the kind of guy to cheat on a test.

I think Draco Malfoy is pretty cool, or would be if he wasn't all talk and actually did some cool stuff.

✳

Tabatha, *Chippenham, Wiltshire, England, 12 years old*

I adore Hermione's name! It's really weird and different, like mine! I think she must be really pretty, with curly brown hair and brown eyes. And I think she would be a great friend. I really liked it when she hit Malfoy. Go Hermione!

3

How We Act Out the Characters in the Books:

Taking on Roles and Inventing New Ones

Let's Pretend is a favorite game of children, and what could be more fun than to pretend to be in one of the Harry Potter adventures? Some children like to invent new characters and situations for the Harry Potter stories. Others have imagined ways to re-create the world of Hogwarts. Still others have participated in Harry Potter parties at home and at school. Here are some of their ideas.

*

Ninon, *Jasper, Arkansas, 12 years old*

I live in Arkansas, but I'd rather live in Denmark or Wales. I really like the Harry Potter books because they are sort of present-day and old-time books at the same time. I usually only read legends or fictional legends.

I would like to say that I think J. K. Rowling's books are equal to those of Tolkien and C. S. Lewis.

I like the Harry Potter books because I can imagine myself into them. I do this in every great book I read. In *The Lord of the Rings,* I am an eleven maid Estel, since Estel means "Hope" and that's my middle name.

In the Harry Potter books, I imagine myself as a Slytherin girl with long black hair and gray-green eyes. I call myself Serpent Angolin, because I change moods faster than thought, which I do in real life. I'm sort of a spy-behind-enemy-lines, though I don't do much.

I feel sorry for Snape because I am an uncool kid, too. I have a temper that might match his. I am also bitter to my rivals, even without reason, but I wish he hadn't told everyone about Lupin.

I think it is stupid that no one will speak Voldemort's name. That is just like Sauron in *The Lord of the Rings*. There's no need to be afraid of a simple name, or even a great name, not even an evil one.

I hope there will be nymphs or dryads or naiads in the future books, and that they use some Danish or Welsh legends. I love them.

I like J. K. Rowling's style. It is funny, dangerous, dry, happy, wise, and funny. No, I did *not* copy that; I figured it out.

∗

Bre, *Madison, Tennessee, 12 years old*

Peeves reminds me of my brother, who acts his shoe size rather than his age, and the only one who can control him is my mom. He even has that devilish way of talking that Peeves has.

I was not a sports player, but ever since Quidditch became a topic of interest to me I joined the soccer team. I got instructions for playing Quidditch on the ground off the Internet.

Every day, my friends Courtney, Amanda, and Brit act out our roles in the Harry Potter stories. Courtney and Amanda are at constant war with me not to say Lord Voldemort's name. For Halloween we are going to be wizards. We prefer to be called wizards, not witches even though that's the proper name for girl wizards. We like "wizard" because "witch" sounds evil.

The end of *Harry Potter and the Goblet of Fire* surprised me a lot. It left me so speechless that all I could say was, and I quote, "Lord Voldemort is back!"

I think that everyone who reads, understands, loves, and takes these books to mind is not a Muggle but a wizard. This may sound corny, but if you do all the things I've listed you have found the magic deep inside of you. And that is the best kind of magic, even if it means having a homemade wand and costume.

✳

Kathleen, *Brighton, Sussex, England, 10 years old*

Sirius is my favorite character. I asked my mum and she said Sirius means something about a star.✳

When I play Harry Potter at school, I am always a girl whose name is Carri. She is Lord Voldemort's daughter and can do really cool Dark Arts, even though she is in Gryffindor. Snape likes her. My friend Jocelene is a girl called Corri. She is in Slytherin and her mum was Lord Voldemort's most faithful servant.

✳

Madeline and Greta, *Lyndhurst, Ohio*

We love the Harry Potter books. We put our heads together and thought it would be a great idea if there could be a Hogwarts for Muggles. People could pay to be a student at this Hogwarts for a week or something. It would have to be built by a forest so there could be a Forbidden Forest. In the forest there could be white horses trained to act like unicorns, dogs trained to act like werewolves, people dressed like vampires, and everything else. There could also be kids dressed up like the characters in the books. We haven't got any ideas on how to make a giant squid (yet).

✳

Katie, *Naperville, Illinois, 13 years old*

I first read the Harry Potter books when I was eleven. Last Halloween I threw a Harry Potter party. We had a Sorting Hat. I made a tape-recording about everybody's personality and stuff so we could be sorted. We played Quidditch with hula hoops and we hid the Snitch in the bushes. Here are some ideas for T-shirts.

✳See the letter from Lauralee and Gus of Clovis, California, page 80, for their information about Sirius, the Dog Star.

Hogwarts' houses. On the front, the house name, and on the back, the description from the Sorting Hat's poem in the first book.

Muggles. On the front, "Muggle." On the back, " 'A Muggle,' said Hagrid, 'it's what we call non-magic folk like them.' "

Harry Potter. On the front, "I love Harry Potter." On the back, a list such as: "Name: Harry Potter/Best friends: Ron, Hermione/Sport: Quidditch/Position: Seeker/Broom: Firebolt/Eye color: Green/Hair color: Black/Crush: Cho Chang."

Place Names. Like Knockturn Alley, Diagon Alley, Flourish and Blotts, Gringotts, Zonko's Joke Shop, the Shrieking Shack.

There could also be T-shirts with poems, rhymes and riddles, Hogwarts' teachers' names, or brands of wizard candy.

➡ *Note: To illustrate her ideas, Katie sent us a batch of tiny T-shirts cut out of paper with lettering on front and back.*

★

Sara, *Barrow upon Humber, North Lincolnshire, England, 12 years old*

I started to read the Harry Potter books before I started secondary school so I was hoping I would get a letter saying I was a witch. I ask myself questions like, "What if?"

My favorite Harry Potter book is the first one because everything is fresh and new. By the second and third ones, you know the way J. K. Rowling writes.

I get so involved with the books I find myself acting out little scenes whilst on my own or speaking passages out loud. My favorite teacher is Professor Snape because without an evil teacher the story would be incomplete.

I solved the puzzle in the first book. It was hard.

∗

Alex, *Fort Wayne, Indiana*

I wish I were Harry, because I could turn people into things. If I could change places with other people I would pick someone perfect in my class.

I really admire Harry. I hate Pokémon and wish it would become extinct.

Sometimes my friend and I call ourselves "Harry" on our school papers.

∗

Hajera, *Clinton Township, Michigan, 9 years old*

Reading *Harry Potter* makes me feel like I am Hermione or Professor McGonagall. I wish I could be Hermione because she's the smart one and she knows her magic.

I finished *Harry Potter* a lot earlier than my class. I always finish books first.

∗

Lindsey, *Woodinville, Washington, 8 years old*

My friends and I have been working on a Harry Potter book we named *Harry Potter and the Secret of the Dementors.* The friends I am working with say that the new Quidditch captain should be called Simms, but I don't really like the name.

∗

Derek, *Frostburg, Maryland, 12 years old*

The Harry Potter books are my favorite books ever! I read the first book in October 1999 and liked it so much that I was Harry Potter for Halloween. My friend was Voldemort and we had a lot of fun. I read the other two books in November on a trip. I liked them even better.

I would hate to get a disgusting-flavored Every Flavor Bean. I would want to get a peach one or one that tastes like my grandma's pineapple-filled cookies.

I think the bad guys are just bad enough, if you know what I mean. The books would have no adventure without them.

It would be awesome to be able to play Quidditch. I think of the flying brooms as the magic world's bicycles.

I want Harry to learn more about his folks and his past.

★

Chelsie, *Ashland, Maine*

Our library teacher said Harry didn't die and he's real. I don't believe her. Her name is Mrs. Gram. Mrs. Gram dressed up as Harry Potter. She looked silly.

My teacher dressed up as the professor. If you want to know what all the dressing up is for, the school had a Harry Potter Day!

★

Jane and Katie, *Ellinwood, Kansas, 10 years old*

We are putting lightning bolts on ourselves. We really like Harry, Ron, Hermione, and Hagrid. We hate the Slytherins. They are *sooo* stupid. We like Professor Flitwick, the Charms teacher.

★

Holly, *Pittsburgh, Pennsylvania, 10 years old*

I love the Harry Potter books. I memorize lines in them. I'm a little like Hermione. I have long brown hair and my personality is a lot like hers. I also like to talk in a British accent. It is natural.

⁕

Sheena, *Sandy Hook, Connecticut*

I love the Harry Potter books and I cannot wait until the next one comes out. I am writing a book named "Riddle Bark and You-Know-Who."

⁕

Libby, *Moonstone, Ontario, Canada*

The Harry Potter books are the best books in the world! My best friend, Mikko, has glasses just like Harry Potter's. I don't have glasses, though. At school, Mikko, Ali (my little sister), and I keep practicing our spells. We really want to increase our knowledge.

⁕

Allison, *San Francisco, California*

I hope Hagrid gets to see Beaky again soon. I hope he gets a new monster! Is Hagrid his last name? He is my second-favorite character in *Harry Potter*. At my friend's house, I am Hagrid and I always have her over for tea. She is Hermione, but we won't get into that.

➡ *Note: According to J. K. Rowling's books, Hagrid is indeed the giant's last name. You'll find his first name on page 48 of the first book when he introduces himself to Harry and the Dursleys.*

⁕

Brittany, *Downsville, Louisiana*

When I am sad and I read one of the Harry Potter books, I feel so much better. Every time I read just one sentence, or one word, I smile really big. I love the part in the third book when Harry tells Snape to shut up about his dad. He sure showed him! Sometimes Hermione made me so sick I wanted to slap her. I think it was very nice of Sirius Black to give Ron his very own owl.

My school, Hillcrest Elementary, did a D.A.R.E. skit in which Harry, Ron, and Hermione showed Ravenclaw, Hufflepuff, and the bad Slytherins about how they should not smoke, drink, or do any type of drugs. Everybody loved it. The guy who played Harry was really good at acting. His hair was messy like Harry's and he even had glasses, but no scar. He had a Nimbus Two Thousand, but it's too bad he didn't have a Firebolt.

✴

Brooke, *Gastonia, North Carolina*

I've read *Harry Potter and the Sorcerer's Stone* thirty-six times, the second book twenty-nine times, and the third forty-four times. I never tire of the Harry Potter books. Some friends and I have taken different roles and made up some characters. I am Hermione, the astrology teacher, and Madam Pomfrey. My friends think I should be Madam Pince. I don't know why. I only read thirty books a week.

My made-up character is Voldia Riddle, You-Know-Who's daughter. She's in Slytherin and she likes Harry and they are friends. Her hair is silky black and she has sapphire eyes. She's also really smart. Voldia doesn't like Ron and hates Hermione so much that she calls her a Mudblood. She doesn't like Malfoy or his friends, either. Many of the boys like her because she is so pretty. I don't play her too much because my friends don't like Voldia. If I really am not in a good mood I will be Voldia Riddle.

I hope the new Defense Against the Dark Arts teacher is a vampire. I also think that there should be more unicorns and dragons.

✴

Taryn, *Peoria, Illinois, 9 years old*

I think it would be neat to build a Hogwarts summer camp. The camp would start at the end of June and end in early August. At the end of every school year a newsletter could be sent home about it, or it could be sent on the Internet. The kids would send in forms saying they'd come. There would be a camp both in the U.K. and in the U.S.

Students would first go to a place like Diagon Alley, with the Leaky Cauldron, Quality Quidditch, and Flourish and Blotts. They'd get their stuff, stay one night in a private parlor, and next day go on a train to Hogwarts and go to the feast. They'd get sorted into dorms, and electronic portraits would ask for passwords. Staff would dress as the teachers and Dumbledore. Kids would pick their classes and get grades and do everything just like the students in the book. Hogsmeade would be a special treat for about a week. No permission slips!

Students would be assigned a name on the seventh day, according to the dorms they were in. A lively boy in Gryffindor would be Harry Potter, a girl who studied hard would be Hermione, and so forth.

∗

Elizabeth, *Pelham Manor, New York*

I love the Harry Potter books because as I'm reading them I picture what's happening inside my head. Reading *Harry Potter* also gives me something to do because at my house it's pretty boring.

I pretend my school is Hogwarts, because it looks like a castle, and my regular teacher is Professor Snape, because he's kind of mean. There are woods surrounding my school, as I picture Hogwarts has.

∗

Carly, *Vienna, West Virginia*

As I read the first Harry Potter book, I fell in love! I went to a Harry Potter party with four friends. We played Quidditch (I got the Snitch) and made witches' brew (water in dry ice), and sang Happy Birthday to Harry.

I think J. K. Rowling is a very creative and excellent writer. I hope to be an author someday. I made a Harry Potter website. I wish that Ms. Rowling would visit it.

∗

Mollie, *Vienna, West Virginia*

I read the fourth Harry Potter book in three days, I loved it so much. Ms. Rowling is a super author. She writes things so realistically; for example, I feel like I'm saying a bad word when I say "Voldemort."

On Harry's birthday, my friends and I had a Harry Potter birthday party. We painted scars on our foreheads and had robes and hats. We played Quidditch and had Bertie Bott's Every Flavor Beans! We guessed what flavor we thought they were. It was fun.

I think Ms. Rowling is a very strong person. She kept going when things weren't going so well in her life. She is not only a fantastic author, but a role model for everyone.

Opinions on Future Books:

What Should, and Should Not, Happen Next

J. K. Rowling has said that she plans to write seven Harry Potter books, one for each year Harry attends Hogwarts School of Witchcraft and Wizardry. But it's hard for her readers to wait patiently a whole year for the next book, because they have some ideas about what they'd like to see happen next. These are some of their ideas.

*

Christabel, *Exeter, Devon, England, 13 years old*

I purchased *We Love Harry Potter!* when buying my fourth Harry Potter book. It was very interesting looking at some very American opinions and comparing them to British ones.

I think that a good and interesting contrast to this book would be another one with English children making their comments and giving their feedback! This would provide American children with an idea of what English children—and their culture—are like.

➥ *Note: You'll find comments from children all over the world in this book.*

*

Ashley, *Crab Orchard, West Virginia, 11 years old*

My favorite characters are Harry and Dobby the house-elf because they are both funny. I gave myself the hiccups because I laughed so hard when Dobby started banging his head on everything.

I like Harry because he is so brave. If I were in some of the predicaments that he was in, I would have wet my pants. I hate snakes and all other reptiles.

At school, we had a day when we were supposed to dress up as our favorite book characters. Almost everyone dressed as Harry Potter. We had one Hagrid.

I really look forward to when the next Harry Potter book comes out, because I am getting surgery in April on my back, and I'll be cooped up all summer. I really would like to see Harry and Hermione fall in love. The only thing the Harry Potter books are missing is a touch of romance.

*

Caroline, *Guildford, Surrey, England, 10 years old*

Ron is my favorite character. It must be hard on him, being pushed into the background, with six siblings. Also, everyone makes such a fuss about Harry and Hermione, they forget about Ron. But I think he's great. He's a bit like me; he has a bad temper, untidy writing, untidy hair, and a soft, kind heart. Also, I hate corned beef and I'm scared stiff of spiders!

I hope Ron doesn't get a girlfriend because I like his strong spirit and a girlfriend would change that. Hermione thinks she's so great; she tells everyone what to do and sticks her nose into other people's business. I don't think much of Harry either; he's a bit of a wuss. I think Ron should stand up to Draco Malfoy. If I were Ron, I'd have smashed his nose in by now!

*

Kymberly, *Coon Rapids, Minnesota*

Harry Potter is the most fascinating boy I have ever heard of. The way most people portray a witch or wizard is as an ugly, pimply, short thing who eats kids for lunch. But once you have read a Harry Potter book, you think of witches and wizards as looking like Harry, Ron, or Hermione.

I think Harry, Ron, and Hermione will be friends for quite a long while, kind of like Sirius Black, James Potter, and Professor Lupin, only longer.

You must admit it is quite amazing how You-Know-Who has managed to stay alive for thirteen years after his defeat by Harry Potter (and his parents). I can understand why everyone hates Malfoy. He's just dumb.

Harry's parents sound so cool, and it would kick if I was related to them. Then I might actually have magic in my blood. I know that in the book *We Love Harry Potter!* there are predictions about what happened to Harry's parents. My prediction is that their spirits live in the mirror of Erised. The reason I think this is because the thing Harry desires most is being with his parents, and the only time he saw his parents was when he found the mirror.

I like Harry's best friends a lot. Hermione is like me: smart and with brown curly hair. Ron is like me, too; we are believers in "divination" and are always the last to do things. And Hagrid: tallest at school and a short annoyance span.

I think Ron and Hermione should go out together, because they despise each other and yet they are best friends. They are perfect for each other!

Dumbledore should stay headmaster and live for 665 years, like his friend Nicholas Flamel. If he does die, he should stay in the castle as a ghost, like the Fat Friar or Peeves. I think that after the seven books come out, more books should come out! Many of my friends agree; we want more books.

∗

Scott, *Ogden, Utah*

I was thinking that Harry Potter's life is very similar to his father's. And I think Neville Longbottom is a lot like Wormtail; they are both very shaky and aren't very good at magic. Ron is a lot like Sirius, and Draco Malfoy is like Snape. But I can't figure out where Hermione and Lupin would fit in.

I think Harry and his friends should become Animagi because they could find out a lot of stuff that they didn't know by changing into an animal. Plus, think of all the times they could have gotten away from Lord Voldemort if they could transform, and he wouldn't know where they went.

> ●+ *Note: Scott's idea about the similarities between certain characters in the Harry Potter books is thought provoking. It's not clear, however, how Ron Weasley resembles Sirius Black, other than the fact that they both wish Harry well. What do other readers think?*

*

Jeddi, *Olongapo City, Philippines*

I'm called Jem for short. I have read the first three Harry Potter books. I read in the book *We Love Harry Potter!* that Harry should have a girlfriend and that his girlfriend might be Cho Chang, the Ravenclaw Quidditch Seeker. I do not agree with that. If they grow up and get married, Cho Chang will be Cho Potter. That name's a yuck!!

Harry should have girlfriend who is a new student at Hogwarts. An intelligent one. It would be better if the girl has long, straight black hair. She should be on the Gryffindor Quidditch team, even their Captain. But if not, it's okay.

I don't want Hermione Granger to be Harry's girlfriend. Hermione could be Ron's girlfriend instead.

*

Stacey, *Ray Township, Michigan, 13 years old*

I love Harry Potter and read all of his books. I just have one thing to say to the characters: *"Are you people nuts?"* Cho Chang should *not* be Harry's girlfriend; Hermione should! Hermione is totally smart, nice, and awesome. Cho Chang should get a life. She was teasing Harry while playing Quidditch!

I wish Hagrid had turned Dudley all the way into a pig!

I would like J. K. Rowling to make Harry actually kill Lord Voldemort!

*

Crystal, San Ramon, California, 11 years old

My favorite character is Harry because he has great courage. I also like Hermione. Ron is okay but I think he is rough. I don't know why people like the Nimbus Two Thousand. I like the Firebolt a lot because it is *sooo* fast. However, I think Harry should change to another broom, maybe a Thunderbolt. Harry should have a beautiful girlfriend in the next book. That would make the book so romantic. I hope that J. K. Rowling writes longer books.

*

Daniel, Brazil, Indiana, 13 years old

The Harry Potter books take you to a whole new world. I can't wait until J. K. Rowling writes more of them. I think someone should make a Harry Potter bookmark to go along with the books.

I think Harry should live with Sirius Black. Black might even teach Harry some magic he knows. I think Snape should be fired or start to like Harry. But then, there wouldn't be a villain.

My favorite of the foods they eat are the Christmas crackers* because you find surprises in them.

*

Amelia, Perth, Australia, 8 years old

I started reading the Harry Potter books when I turned seven. I just can't keep my nose out of them! I think Percy should be the Dark Arts teacher. My favorite animal is a hippogriff. I'm asking my mum to get me a hippogriff for my birthday!

---

*Christmas crackers are not actually food. They are party favors that make a cracking sound when pulled open.

*

Alexandria, *Sparks, Nevada*

I hope that when Harry gets a girlfriend it's Hermione, because she is Muggle-born and it makes sense. I hope to read more about Harry's parents, especially his mother. Sometimes I think she never existed. In the next book I hope Harry does something stupid, like always, but as long as Harry gets into trouble in future books it's fine with me. I hope to read the British version as well.

*

Harry, *New York, New York*

I would like to ask J. K. Rowling to make an eighth book of Harry Potter so we know what Harry does as a fully trained wizard.

*

Lauralee and her son, Gus, *Clovis, California, 7 years old*

My son Gus and I were just reading about constellations and learned that there is one called Canis Major, or "the Big Dog," also called "the Dog Star," after one of Orion's hunting dogs, Sirius. We remembered that Sirius Black is an Animagus who can take the shape of a dog! We wonder if J. K. Rowling is interested in astronomy, too, and if any other astronomical characters will show up in future books?

> ➥ *Note: As a fantasy writer, J. K. Rowling is undoubtedly familiar with many myths and legends, including those the Greeks and Romans used to name the stars. If you look closely, you might recognize some other references to astronomy in her books. Many of the names she gives her characters can be traced to such myths and to myths from the Norsemen, medieval Europeans, ancient Egyptians, and others. For examples, see Chapter 14: Myths and Legends.*

*

Anonymous, *Medina, Ohio*

I totally disagree with people who say Hermione is a pest, just because she is smart and shows off. She probably doesn't realize she is showing off. I don't realize it whenever I show off.

I think Harry's father worked in Diagon Alley and Harry's mother was probably a teacher at Hogwarts (maybe Defense Against the Dark Arts). I'd like to see more about Harry's mother.

I'd like to see Fred and George blow up the Potions lab.

I'd like to see Harry lose a Quidditch match. Being undefeated is too perfect. You have to lose sometime. If Harry's team does lose one game, it shouldn't be because of Harry. They might just not score enough points with the Quaffle. I'd like to see Harry become a pro Quidditch player or Headmaster (or, as we call it in the U.S.A., "principal") of Hogwarts. I'd like to see Harry marry Hermione and have a girl and a boy. I hope that when Harry's son goes to Hogwarts he will do something really great.

I'd like to see students playing instruments at Hogwarts.

I'd like to see Ron become a prefect, because I can relate to him trying to live up to his brothers (I have three sisters).

➡ *Note: Harry did lose a Quidditch match, to Hufflepuff, in* Harry Potter and the Prisoner of Azkaban.

*

William, *Allesley, Coventry, Warwickshire, England, 9 years old*

In the eighth book, Sirius Black could come to the Dursleys and turn them into pigs. Then Black could take Harry to live with him in a faraway wood where the Azkaban guards can't find them and they live happily ever after.

*

Miranda, *Athens, Pennsylvania*

I think Dobby should be in future books, and I also hope that, like it says in the third book, dragons should be at the entrance of Hogwarts and one of them should be Norbert. Draco Malfoy is funny, but I wish he could be even funnier. J. K. Rowling shouldn't stop making the Harry Potter books after the seventh one.

*

Mara, *London, Ontario, Canada, 9 years old*

My teacher, Mr. MacDonald, is reading *Harry Potter and the Chamber of Secrets* to us. I figured out who opened the Chamber. I think the next book should be about Harry dropping out of school to join a professional Quidditch team.

➽ *Note: Mara is the only child we've heard from who has suggested that Harry drop out of Hogwarts in future J. K. Rowling books!*

*

Andrea, *Terre Haute, Indiana, 9 years old*

I'm a huge fan of J. K. Rowling's work. I think all her books are brilliant. I want to become an author when I grow up.

I have a hundred questions about what happens in the next Harry Potter books. Will seven books answer them all? I hope this inspires Ms. Rowling to write more books. And when she's finished writing Harry Potter books, I hope she makes some of her other books about witches and wizards.

*

Jennifer, *San Mateo, California*

I hope that in the fifth Harry Potter book, J. K. Rowling will make Voldemort scarier than ever. I hope Hermione can have the

Time-Turner back. I think it could be quite useful. In the seventh book, I would like to see Voldemort die, and Hermione marry Harry. Then, after the series is finished, I would like Ms. Rowling to tell Hermione's and Ron's side of the story in diary form. I hope J. K. Rowling becomes a billionaire doing the things she loves!

∗

Siofra, *Winston Salem, North Carolina, 9 years old*

Harry is my favorite, and when he grows up he should be the Defense Against the Dark Arts professor.

∗

Farin, *Dixon, Illinois, 12 years old*

I'm a really big fan of J. K. Rowling. I was wondering if she would write eight books instead of seven, because I want to know what happens to the characters after Hogwarts.

∗

Orla, *County Dublin, Ireland*

My favorite creatures are the nifflers, Madame Olympe's huge horses, the owls, and hippogriffs. I like Sirius, even though he's a bit protecting over Harry; I can understand him, because Harry has encountered Voldemort four times already!

Since Voldemort came back, it would be cool for Harry by special allowance from the Ministry of Magic to become an Animagus to hide from Voldemort, because the Fidelius Charm didn't work. I want Sirius to get his name cleared so Harry can live with him instead of the Dursleys (it's getting boring at the start of the books). I know Cho Chang is going to be Harry's girlfriend and Krum is Hermione's boyfriend, and I don't think Padma is going to be Ron's, so who's Ron's?

➡ *Note: What kind of animal would Harry turn into as an Animagus? Perhaps a hawk, because he's described by J. K. Rowling as a quick and agile flyer. What do other readers think?*

✳

Amanda, *Pleasant Hill, California, 11 years old*

I think Harry should have a girlfriend like Hermione. Ron should have Cho Chang as his girlfriend because they both love Quidditch.

✳

Jill, *Albany, California, 12 years old*

I have a question. In the book *We Love Harry Potter!* Becky Rubin wrote that Mrs. Norris died. I thought she just got petrified.

I think that Harry's girlfriend should be Cho Chang, even though it would break Ginny's heart. I am curious to see who the new Quidditch Captain will be, now that Wood is gone.

I heard a rumor that there might be a college series. Is there such a thing as Wizard college?

➡ *Note: Mrs. Norris was indeed petrified, not dead as it at first appeared, as you can see on page 142 of* Harry Potter and the Chamber of Secrets.

So far, J. K. Rowling has not mentioned a wizard college. However, many of her fans would like to see the series continued after Harry and his friends leave Hogwarts, so who knows?

✳

Debbie, *Newberry, Florida, 12 years old*

In future books, I think Harry should marry a beautiful girl with golden hair, a nice personality, and a great talent for Quidditch, but I think she should also save his life somehow.

I think Ron and Hermione should get married, Ron become a Minister of Magic and Hermione a professor at Hogwarts.

I'm Scottish and I hope to see J. K. Rowling on my trip back to the home country of my ancestors. I even have some relatives there. I hope she comes out with more books soon and I hope that Harry Potter lives forever.

★

Michelle, *Manchester, Lancashire, England, 13 years old*

When I ordered *Harry Potter and the Goblet of Fire,* I was pleased to receive a free copy of a book entitled *We Love Harry Potter!* After finishing reading the Harry Potter book (which took only three days as I couldn't put it down!) I flicked through the other book. It was very interesting, but I couldn't help noticing that, in a chapter on Harry's parents, I found that J. K. Rowling was thinking of bringing Harry's parents back into the future books. I don't think this is a very good idea.

For one thing, Harry is only famous because he is the only person ever to survive Voldemort's curses, and if his parents lived as well then he wouldn't be the only person, would he? Also, I am sure Dumbledore would know they were alive and wouldn't have sent Harry to the Dursleys if he could help it. Another thing is that Sirius Black and Hagrid arrived when Voldemort had left Harry's house and I think they would have told him if his parents were alive.

➻ *Note: Michelle has the instincts of an author! Hers are probably the very reasons why J. K. Rowling did not bring Harry's parents back to life. The chapter about Harry's parents in* We Love Harry Potter! *was based on children's theories about them, before any of them had read* Harry Potter and the Goblet of Fire, *and not on any knowledge of J. K. Rowling's intentions.*

*

Erica, *Luther, Iowa*

In future books, I would like to have Harry Potter hired as the Defense Against the Dark Arts teacher (he has plenty of experience). Then, when Dumbledore retires, they will hire Harry to be headmaster. I also think that Harry and Hermione will stay together after they are out of school and finally get married.

Ron and his family will eventually get rich enough so they don't have any money problems, but not overly rich. Then they just wouldn't be the same.

*

Isabelle, *Sydney, Australia*

I love how J. K. Rowling puts lots of red herrings and twists in her books.

In future books, I think Sirius or Lupin should become the new Defense Against the Dark Arts teacher because Snape can't keep his big mouth shut about Sirius. Harry should go to live with Sirius, and Padfoot should come and get Harry from the Dursleys just to give them a fright.

Malfoy, Crabbe, Goyle, and Pansy Parkinson should (if they don't get expelled) be held back a year.

*

Phoebe, *Ffynore, Swansea, Wales, 12 years old*

I hate the Dursleys. They are absolutely horrid. I don't like Dobby, the house-elf, in the second book (I'm the only one so far that I know of who doesn't!) because if it hadn't been for Dobby, Harry and Ron wouldn't have got into so much trouble by using the flying car. But I have to admit that Dobby is quite a character, and very pitiful.

I find it a bit annoying that people won't say Voldemort's name in the book, because it embarrasses Harry when *he* says it.

I think there should be more unicorns in the books.

In the next book, I think that Harry and Ron should have girlfriends, Hermione for Harry, and Cho Chang or someone for Ron. Ron and Hermione just wouldn't go, because they are always fighting. I think that Harry should stick up for her a bit more; it is rather hard being a swat* sometimes (and I should know).

I would like to see Lupin make a comeback.

I'd like to go to Hogwarts. I'd like to be in Gryffindor, and I know one thing, my mum and dad would certainly sign my permission slip for Hogsmeade. I think that Hermione and I would get along well.

In one of the next books, I think that we should find out what Dumbledore's vision is when he looks into the mirror of Erised. If there were such a thing as a mirror of Erised in our Muggle world, I bet we'd all want to know what was there. Magic only comes when we have a deep imagination. You don't have to be a wizard to know that.

∗

Sarah, *Paoli, Indiana*

I think that Albus Dumbledore should find out that Harry has a twelve-year-old sister who is living with Muggles. This girl should be named Sarah Beth. She should have brown hair and blue eyes. Sarah should be a witch. Sirius Black should go on Buckbeak and take her to Hogwarts. She would be one or two years behind because the Muggles didn't let her read the letter telling her to come to Hogwarts. Hagrid can get the stuff that she needs for school. Sarah's birthday is on September 10. She doesn't know how to write with a feather. She doesn't know a lot of things. But she has read the four Harry Potter books. She is a magical princess.

*A swat is someone who studies a lot.

In a later letter, Sarah writes:

I think Hermione should put a tickle charm on Snape at a party. Then he will be nice.

I think Harry should do a very bad tickle charm on Draco Malfoy.

I hope that Sirius Black never gets caught.

∗

James, *Canandaigua, New York, 10 years old*

I think the Harry Potter books are the greatest children's books ever. I also like all the pictures made by Mary Grandpré. I think all of the covers are the coolest-looking ones I've ever seen.

If there are going to be more books, and I know there are, there should be more pictures in them (even though it's fun to imagine what they look like).

∗

Rob, *Winter Garden, Florida*

When Harry marries, he should marry Hermione. She would be excellent.

How do you get chosen to go to Hogwarts? Could someone ask Mr. Dumbledore if I can come, okay?

I'd like to tell Hermione that I think she's cute.

∗

Sophie, *Cheadle, Staffordshire, England, 9 years old*

I have a couple of titles for J. K. Rowling's next books. Here they are:

Harry Potter and . . .
  "the Crystal of Stone"
  "the Cave of Herbs"

"the Box into Heaven"
"the Ghosts of His Parents."

*

Candy, *Covington, Kentucky, 10 years old*

Harry Potter books are nonstop action. They are filled with wonderful things that make you want to be Harry. I like Hagrid's accent and hope in the following books I find out about his past. In the next books I hope Harry does get a girlfriend. I hope it is Ginny. I also hope Hermione gets a boyfriend.

*

Justin, *Sheffield, Massachusetts, 9 years old*

I love the Harry Potter books. In the next book I want tons and tons of Quidditch. Maybe the author should put in some gargoyles. I know there haven't been any in the books so far, but maybe she should add some.

✳

Monica, *Gulf Breeze, Florida, 8 years old*

My mom and I read the first Harry Potter book together because it was too hard for me to read by myself. I like all the characters except the Dursleys. I would not like to go to Hogwarts because I would miss my mommy and daddy.

I would like to know more about Harry's parents and why Voldemort killed them. My mom and I thought maybe they had the Sorcerer's Stone hidden in their basement to do some very important testing, which would explain why Voldemort was after them. Voldemort put a spell on them that took them back in time for one hundred years, or maybe he turned them into frogs for twenty years. Maybe Harry can eventually be reunited with his parents. And maybe Harry has some brothers and sisters he doesn't know about. That would be pretty exciting.

✳

Ben, *Bristol, England, 9 years old*

I really loved all the Harry Potter books. I hope there are going to be a fifth, sixth, and seventh year at Hogwarts. I would like to say to J. K. Rowling, "Please do not give up! It is the best book ever written in Britain."

✳

Julie, *County Offaly, Ireland*

I think Hagrid should fall in love. He is so lonely and needs a wife and kids.

Snape should leave his job to work in the U.S.A. and Black should get the job and, of course, should have his name cleared of all things said about him. I disagree with the person who said Malfoy should leave; he makes it interesting. If Harry has no enemy, it's boring, and if everything is happy all the time, what's the point in that?

*

Lindsay, *Courtice, Ontario, Canada*

I think Hermione is very cool and very smart. This dorky person I know thinks she and Ron make a great couple! Hah! Yeah, right, in her dreams, maybe!

I think in the next book, Harry should blow up Vernon Dursley and Aunt Petunia. Dudley deserves to be blown up, too, but we wouldn't want Harry to get a bad reputation! Dudley should be sent to an orphanage with a dungeon with rats and bird plops on the windows.

*

Kyle, *Annapolis County, Nova Scotia, Canada, 12 years old*

My favorite Harry Potter book is the fourth one because it is very long and you spend more time reading and enjoying it. One of my friends and I were wondering whether Professor Moody is going to stay at Hogwarts or not. I think he won't and my friend thinks he will.

➤ *Note: It's hard to decide after reading about the Professor's state of mind on page 720, at the end of that book. We will have to wait and see, when the next books are published!*

Letters to Characters in the Books:

What We'd Like to Say to Harry, Hermione, Ron, and the Rest

The people in the Harry Potter books are so vivid that a reader feels as if he actually knows them. So it's not surprising that many children like to write to them, as if they actually existed. Here are some of the kids' letters.

*

Joseph, *Ackworth, Georgia, 10 years old*

My friend Robert and I got the whole fourth grade class into reading the Harry Potter books. We even made chemistry sets to pretend we were making potions.

Here's what I would like to write to Harry: Does Dudley have pneumonia? How's Hedwig? Enough questions. I might be going to Pigwarts in two years. I've been going to Miagon Alley lately. These are the American wizard hideouts. I wish you could come to my house; we'd have a blast. You know, I am planning to curse the Dursleys. Well, *I'm* not; my dad is.

Here's what I would write to Albus Dumbledore: How have you been? I've been fine, but what stinks is I have to go to an all-Muggle school.

And here's what I would write to Sirius Black: I have found

your hiding place. Don't worry; I'm clean. Call me if you need food or lodging.

✶

Justin, *Walterboro, South Carolina, 13 years old*

Here is a letter I've written to Professor Snape.

Dear Professor Severus Snape,
    I am sure you don't get that much mail since everyone hates you. So I am writing to you. I am a Harry Potter fan and I have read the books to my younger brothers. I am waiting for the fifth book to come out.
    P.S. I know Harry Potter is not real!

✶

Mark, *Muskegon, Michigan*

Here is a letter I would like to send to Harry Potter.

Dear Harry,
    Waz up? You have such a cool life; I wish I could be you. Are you planning on ever sending a letter with Hedwig? I mean, you barely ever send letters. You really should go out with Cho Chang, or at least get a girlfriend. Hermione really gets on your nerves sometimes, doesn't she? You should be more careful about school, otherwise you're going to get expelled.

✶

Bethany, *Courtice, Ontario, Canada, 10 years old*

I hate how the Dursleys treat Harry; they should be put in jail for wizard abuse! I think Harry should tell Professor Dumbledore to hide behind a corner to watch while Malfoy teases Harry. Ha-ha, serve him right! I think Harry should teach Hagrid to speak properly (not that I mind his speech now). I'd like to tell that awfully strict Professor McGonagall to get a life!

Here's a letter to Fred and George.

Dear Fred and George,

You are my (two of them) favorite characters. I love how you always play tricks on people and I laughed when you said [to Ginny, as they boarded the train to Hogwarts in the first book], "We'll send you a Hogwarts toilet seat!" That was funny! You don't associate much with Hermione, do you? Do you think she's smart?

*

Sung, *Bellevue, Washington*

Here's a letter I'd like to send to Malfoy.

Dear Malfoy,

I say you should be nicer to Harry. You'll be looking at him someday and you will be thinking, "Why was I so mean to Harry?" If you change your heart about him, you people can get along. Be nice to Harry's friends, too.

*

Ross, *Ashton, Australia, 11 years old*

In the third book, I thought Malfoy should have gotten detention.

In the fourth book, when Dumbledore gave the speech about Cedric and how kind he was, I nearly started crying.

At school, my friends and I make wands and duel. I have every curse written down except a couple for which the book doesn't give the magic words.

I would like to ask Harry what it is like to have no parents and then see them in the mirror of Erised?

Here is a letter I wrote to Moaning Myrtle.

Dear Myrtle,

It must be really sad being lonely and having no friends. I don't have many friends myself. I don't think people should have the right to tease you. You should be treated as an equal by everyone else.

Maybe you should stop hanging around the girls' toilet and be friends with Peeves and be a poltergeist, or you could just be friends with Nearly Headless Nick or someone like that.

What is it like to die?

∗

Craig, *Strathaven, Scotland*

Here's a letter I wrote to Harry Potter.

Dear Harry,

I am glad you survived the Dark Lord. I bet you were terrified when he arrived at your house. I think your father, James Potter, was so brave when he tried to defend you and your mother, Lily Potter.

Now let's forget about your past and let's think what you have now. You have Hogwarts, a godfather, Hedwig, and best of all Quidditch!

∗

Tia, *Sammamish, Washington, 13 years old*

I've read *Harry Potter* a hundred times (no kidding) and it's so annoying when everyone wants Snape to be fired and Malfoy to be expelled. If they were gone, who would be Harry's antagonist?

And what about Hermione? Everyone thinks she's annoying, too, but how would Harry get along without her?

I've been to Germany, France, Switzerland, and Italy, and while I was at these places I could not find one Harry Potter book, and I looked *everywhere*. I didn't go to those places just for a Harry Potter book, but I was a little disappointed when I couldn't find them.

I am starting my own Harry Potter club on-line and it should be lots of fun!

Sometimes I wonder what it would be like if I was a wizard yet nobody knew. That would be exciting. Then I could move away and live at Hogwarts so I could be with friends, not family. I mean, I could still write to my family but I wouldn't be with them twenty-four hours a day, seven days a week.

I wrote the following letter to Ron Weasley.

Dear Ron,

I think you need to lighten up! What do you think it was like for Hermione when you accused her cat of killing your rat? I bet you felt pretty bad when the truth came out. Boy, do I feel stupid writing to a person who is not even alive, but who cares. I think that of all the people in Hogwarts, I would marry your brother

Fred. I love how he can be funny, caring, sweet, and smart. I pick Fred over George because Fred's funnier. Hey, I think you're cute, too, and I think you and Hermione should get married (sorry if I made you blush).

★

Ashley, *Sammamish, Washington*

The reason I like *Harry Potter* so much is because it lets me explore an area in my mind I never get to when I'm doing anything else. It's like my own little world. Sometimes I wish I could just fall into the pages, as in *Harry Potter and the Chamber of Secrets.* When I'm having a really bad day, I just hop into bed and start reading, and it seems all my troubles just go away. I hope that everyone who's read the Harry Potter series loves it as much as I do.

➤ *Note: The previous two letters were sent from the same address, and the two girls have very similar handwriting. But the letters were written on very different stationery (Tia's has a flowery frame, and Ashley's has a dreamy seascape border).*

∗

Tanner, *Mesa, Arizona, 11 years old*

Here is letter I wrote to Ginny Weasley.

Dear Ginny,

I think you are cute and you should tell Harry you like him. How come Ron is always telling you to go away? By the way, I'm a boy, just so you know. Your mom sounds nice. Tell her I would like a sweater. They sound comfortable.

Have you ever seen a unicorn? I have a good picture of one. I love to read books like *The Lion, the Witch and the Wardrobe* and *A Wrinkle in Time.* Do you?

∗

Nicole, *Arlington Heights, Illinois*

Here's a letter I wrote to Ron.

Dear Ron,

Why do you and Hermione always fight? I think you and Harry are really smart; Hermione is just showing off. Why did you name the minute owl that Sirius Black gave you Pigwidgeon? I think you should have named it Speedy or Errol Junior.

I think you should give Malfoy a bloody nose. Malfoy is so stupid.

When Viktor Krum came to Hogwarts for the Triwizard Tournament, why didn't you just ask for his autograph then? Instead of before he left?

Fleur was pretty. I see why you had a crush on her.

I think you're funny.

∗

Smiley, *Dallas, Georgia, 10 years old*

Here's a letter I wrote to Harry Potter.

Dear Harry,

Do you have a crush on Hermione Granger? Do you like Hogwarts? Do you like me? I love the Harry Potter books. Did you write them yourself? Are you real?

∗

Rosie, *Winchester, Hampshire, England, 11 years old*

Here is a letter I have written to Tom Riddle.

Dear Tom,

I chose to write to you for three reasons: one, because I knew not many others would; two, because I enjoyed reading about you more than anyone else in *Harry Potter and the Chamber of Secrets*; and three, because I don't often come across such good characters, in spite of all of the books I've read. I'm quite an advanced reader and I've read things like *The Lord of the Rings* and *A Wizard of Earthsea,* but they're not so much my sort of book. I like fantasy and fiction that's fast-paced with plenty of humor and a bit out of the ordinary, and that's *Harry Potter.*

I wish I could use my name in an anagram. I bet I can't, but then, I've never tried. Your anagram is really good, but is "Marvolo" a real name?

I'm glad Hogwarts is in Britain, because I'm English and even if I never go to wizard school, I can still do my best to learn Latin or something.

●▶ *Note: "Marvolo" is a name made up by author J. K. Rowling, and it surely does sound like a real name, but you won't find it in many telephone books!*

∗

Rachel, *Lynn, Michigan*

I think the Dursleys are afraid of Harry. I don't like any of the Defense Against the Dark Arts teachers except Lupin. I think the next Defense Against the Dark Arts teacher should be a woman.

My favorite house is Slytherin, except that I don't like Malfoy. I don't really understand the Sorting Hat's decision about Neville Longbottom. He should be in Hufflepuff.

I think you couldn't play Quidditch on the ground without changing it so much it wouldn't be Quidditch anymore. I don't think anyone is a Muggle unless they really hate magic or are afraid of it.

Here's a letter I wrote to Professor McGonagall.

Dear Professor McGonagall,

I think it must be fun to learn Transfiguration in your class, to turn your desk into a pig and back! If I could be an Animagus, I would turn into a hawk. A cat would be fun, too. It's good that you don't favor Gryffindor, because that's what Snape does [he favors Slytherin]. But maybe you shouldn't have given them a big pile of homework the day before Double Potions with the Slytherins. Also, maybe you shouldn't be so hard on Lee Jordan. Just because you find it easy to be fair to all houses, he might favor Gryffindor because, after all, it's his house! I still think you're a good teacher, though.

Your Would-be Student,
Rachel

*

Kendra, *Yukon, Oklahoma, 9 years old*

Here's my letter to Hermione.

Dear Hermione,

I think you are the coolest. My favorite part was when you slapped Draco Malfoy. I can't believe that Harry and Ron didn't believe you slapped him. You're a girl, aren't you? I wish you were real so I could be your friend.

My friends and I are putting on a play. We are taping it. I play Hermione. My friend Jordan is playing Harry Potter (they are both cute).

I'll bet it's cool to be the best witch in Hogwarts. I'll bet you could beat You-Know-Who. Your mood changes so much, you never know what you're going to do or say. Too bad you don't play Quidditch. You could plan the strategy.

➻ *Note: Actually, Harry and Ron saw Hermione slap Malfoy, and tried to stop her from doing it again. But, as Kendra says, they were indeed surprised.*

Games We Like to Play:

Quidditch and More Quidditch

S ince the very first Harry Potter book was published, readers have been fascinated by Quidditch. By now, it's often
played on playgrounds and in backyards by children who
experiment with different ways of playing the ground version of
this high-flying sport. Here are some of their comments, about
Quidditch and about the books in general.

*

Kelsey, *Stilwell, Kansas, 9 years old*

I tried to play Quidditch, but I just can't find anyone who
wants to play. I also can't find a broom.

If Harry ever needs some help with Muggle Studies, he can call
on me and my friends.

*

Joshua, *Brooklyn, New York*

I have a simple way of playing Quidditch. First, you have to
play on an open field. On each team there are three Chasers, one
Keeper, Beaters, and one Seeker. For the Bludgers you can use

basketballs, and the Beaters throw them. For the Quaffle, you can use a soft baseball or handball. And, last, the Snitch will be a person who runs through the field every two minutes until he or she gets caught.

I also invented a board game that I called Quidditch.

✶

Daniel, *Berkeley, California, 5 years old*

A great Quidditch strategy would be to make the Firebolt go *over* the Bludgers, so you would not get hit. Then dodge the other players to catch the Golden Snitch.

I hope in the next book Professor Severus Snape turns into a frog, because he's so mean.

✶

Alex, *Albuquerque, New Mexico, 9 years old*

My favorite character is Harry because he has neat adventures. It was cool when Fred and George Weasley "improved" Percy's head boy badge into "Bighead Boy!" I also like the Marauder's Map. It was a good troublemaking idea.

I wonder where Sirius Black lives?

I wish I was an Animagus. I would turn into a hippogriff and fly around and listen to secret spells and charms.

I would love to play Quidditch. I would be a Chaser because I'm really good at basketball, and being a Chaser you have to shoot the Quaffle into the hoops that the goalkeeper guards. I am not very good at catching small balls so I wouldn't be very good as Seeker. I'm a pretty good goalie in soccer so I'd be good as Keeper in Quidditch. I would be good as a Beater because I'm good at baseball, and a Beater's job is to hit the Bludgers (the balls that try to knock you off your broom).

*

Renato, *Jersey City, New Jersey, 11 years old*

Here is a fun way to play Quidditch. There is an option of broomsticks. I made new and fun rules.

EQUIPMENT
1 basketball (Quaffle)
2 very large beach balls (Bludgers)
1 very small rubber ball (Golden Snitch)
1 bat for each Beater
1 net for each Keeper
A big court with three basketball hoops on each side

OUTFITS
The Seeker needs a pair of Rollerblades, pads, and helmet.
The Beaters wear Rollerblades, pads, and helmets and carry
    bats.
The Keepers wear ordinary clothes or team colors, and each
    holds a net.
The Chasers wear ordinary clothes or team colors.
You can use broomsticks but it will be hard to play.

RULES
1. A coin is flipped to see which team starts.
2. The referee starts by throwing the Quaffle (basketball) in the air. The Chasers dribble the ball and try to shoot it into the hoops. Each successful shot is worth 10 points.
3. The Keepers catch the Quaffle in their nets and throw it back to the players.
4. The Beaters hit the opposing teammates with the Bludgers (beach balls). If a player gets hit with a Bludger, he or she stops in his or her tracks and stays like that until he or she gets hit again.
5. The only players who *cannot* be frozen are the Keepers and Beaters.

6. The referee then throws the Golden Snitch into the court. Then the Seeker comes out. He or she skates around to find the Snitch. (The smaller the ball the more challenging is it for the Seeker to find.)

7. If a player besides the Seeker finds the Snitch, he or she must bounce the Snitch to keep it moving. A player cannot pass the Snitch to the Seeker.

As you know, the game ends when the Snitch is caught. The team that catches the Snitch wins 150 points. The team with the most points wins.

I hope you like my way of playing Quidditch!

★

Renée, Roanoke, Texas, 13 years old

My parents think I'm obsessed with the Harry Potter books. If it has to do with Harry Potter, I am involved in it. I am surprised that the Harry Potter books are so popular. I went to two bookstores that have books with signs that say, "If you like *Harry Potter,* read these," but I think they are dull.

Quidditch is so awesome. I would love to have a Firebolt. I keep telling my little brother to read the books and see if he could help me invent a broomstick. He kept refusing, but when I got the book *We Love Harry Potter!* he changed his mind.

★

Caroline, Lafayette, Louisiana, 9 years old

I go to an all-girls school and almost everyone in my class has read the Harry Potter books. We play *Harry Potter* at recess and my friends are all characters in the books. I always play Ron because he is my favorite. I think he does a great job of telling Hermione off, just like I do to my friend Meghan. I think Ron must have in-

herited comedy from his brothers Fred and George. It's too bad
that Ron doesn't get to play Quidditch.

At my school we have Quidditch games for the whole lower
school once or twice a week. I am Captain of the Gryffindor team.
I do not play as Oliver Wood, though; I play as Ron Weasley. We
changed a few of the players' names. I am a Beater. We still have
only seven players on each team. I made all of the balls and the
clubs for the Beaters on each team. The Quaffle that I made is a
soccer ball painted red. Two large baseballs painted black are the
Bludgers. A tennis ball painted gold is the Snitch. For the Snitch's
wings I took a Ziploc bag and cut out two wings and painted both
of them white. Then I hot-glued the wings onto the tennis ball. So
there you have it, a perfect Quidditch set! We play by the same
rules, only we are not on broomsticks. People throw the balls out
when the person who is playing Madam Hooch tells them to.

7 ✷

Recipes for Wizard Food:

How to Make Magical Food

The dishes served at Hogwarts sound odd but delicious. Many children say they would like to try the food, especially treacle fudge, butterbeer, and pumpkin juice. Some love the Every Flavor Beans, but others are afraid of getting the worst kind of flavors. Some kids have gone to the trouble of figuring out how to make the dishes that appeal to them most. Here are their recipes, along with their thoughts about the books.

*

Claire, *County Cork, Ireland, 15 years old*

I love the endings in each book most of all. The person helping Lord Voldemort is usually the one least suspected. There's a tense mood as a climax is reached.

book was the fourth one. It had 636 which is almost twice the size of the other books in the series, so it's twice as exciting! After the film based on *Harry Potter* is made, more people who weren't reading them before will start reading Harry Potter books, hopefully. After that, it might encourage non-readers to read more often and become more knowledgeable.

I would like to write a letter to Malfoy, because I think it's time that someone besides Harry stood up to him. I'd like to tell him that it's he who's got the problem, not anyone else. In future books, I hope he gets turned into a ferret [as Professor Moody did to him in the fourth book] more often, or else that we find out a secret about him, giving the story a twist.

Finally! I have figured out how to make real pumpkin juice easily—easily, that is, if you have an automatic juicer at home. All you have to do is cut a pumpkin open and take out all the seeds. Then scoop out the flesh with a spoon and place it in the machine. Follow the instructions on the juicing machine and in no time at all you shall have fresh pumpkin juice. If you carve out the pumpkin carefully you could pour the juice inside and use a soup ladle to serve it—perfect for Halloween!

*The American version of the fourth book is 734 pages long, but both versions are essentially the same (a few words were changed to make it easier for American children to read).

✳

Larissa, *White Haven, Pennsylvania, 11 years old*

I love the way all of the characters in the Harry Potter books have their own way of doing things. I don't have a favorite Harry Potter book, although I did feel very sorry for Harry in the first book.

Everyone says Harry is different from the other wizards because of the scar on his forehead that he got from Lord Voldemort. I agree with that, but I am a little like Harry in some ways. I have green eyes just like him, and two scars on my left arm.

I admire Ron for sticking up for everyone. I felt sorry for Hermione when Rita Skeeter wrote bad things about her.

In all my life, I have never had any food as tasty as Chocolate Frogs. To make them, take some Hershey's chocolate bars (plain) and melt them in a dish in a microwave. Then, set frog cookie cutters on a cookie tray and pour the melted chocolate into the cookie cutters. (It takes two or three bars to fill one of the frog cookie cutters I have.) Freeze them until they are hard and thick. Use a knife to cut out the frog from each cookie cutter. For fun, you can wrap a frog and a baseball card in foil and give it to another Harry Potter lover.

Even though I live in the Muggle world, Quidditch is my favorite sport. I like it so much that I made a Firebolt broomstick and tried playing Quidditch with it. I don't know how Harry does it, because it is very hard being the Seeker. But of course I am not as experienced as Harry is.

If you want to make a Firebolt broomstick, just follow these easy directions.

First, get a very long paper or plastic tube, perhaps from inside a wide roll of paper. Next, paint it black and let it dry.

Get some heavy straw and spray-paint it black or any other color you want. Then, use a rubber band to attach the straw in a bunch to one end of the tube.

Use a white crayon to write in fancy letters "Firebolt" on your stick.

I also made a wizard's hat and an owl. They required patterns and sewing.

*

Leanne and Emily, *Cincinnati, Ohio, 10½ years old*

We have succeeded in making a good recipe for butterbeer. You need:

1 cup root beer
A mug
A microwave
A little bit of butter
2 butter-rum Life Savers
⅛ teaspoon warm water
A spoon

Pour the root beer into the mug. Then put it in the microwave for 1 minute. Put the Life Savers into the heated root beer. Wait for them to dissolve (it may take a while). Next, put in the water and add the bit of butter. Stir it up. It should start to fizz. When it stops fizzing, you can drink it. This serves one person. Enjoy!

✳

Dylan, *Springfield, Illinois, 10 years old*

Once I tried to make butterbeer. It took me hours to make it perfect, but I did it, finally. Here's the recipe (makes one serving).

1 bottle root beer
¼ cup cream
1 tablespoon butter, melted

Heat the root beer and cream separately, then stir them together and stir in the butter. You don't have to have cream; it's still really yummy.

8

Poems and Songs We've Written:

Rhymes and Rhythms About Potterisms

There's something mysteriously important about poems, and the Harry Potter stories are certainly full of mystery and important things! So it seems natural to make up poems and songs about them. Here are some rhymes that children have written.

*

Kirby, *Moore, Oklahoma, 12 years old*

Here is my poem about Harry Potter.

HARRY POTTER

Harry Potter has a scar
Upon his forehead.
It was put there by the Dark Lord,
Whose name should not be said.

Harry Potter goes to Hogwarts.
It is a wizard school.
He learns to do lots of spells,
Even one that makes you drool.

Harry Potter has no parents,
But that's okay, you see.
He has a good godfather,
Who's nice as he can be.

He's got two best friends.
They like the rules to bend,
So they can sneak around school.
They'll be with him until the end.

Harry Potter's school,
Which is not at all poor,
Has a very nice headmaster,
His name is Dumbledore.

Harry has a friend named Hagrid,
Who's very nice, you see.
He's a half giant,
And as tall as he can be.

Harry Potter has a crush.
I cannot tell you her name,
Because the rest of his life
Might not be the same.

Now as I end the poem,
There are some things I left out.
You will have to read the books,
C'mon, don't pout.

Please do not plead,
Cry, whine, or sigh,
Because now I have to tell you
Good-bye!

∗

Susie, *Lock Haven, Pennsylvania*

I'd like to know where I can buy a cloak. I can't find one anywhere. Where can I get some magic books? That's been keeping me down, too. I've been keeping an eye out for a wand. I did find a wand that's about ten inches long and gives me a warm feeling. I wish I wasn't such a Muggle.

Hogwarts is my little world I keep to myself. I've urged my brother and sister to read the books and they have. The thing about the Harry Potter books is that when he's in a major mess I have to read on, even if it means not sleeping at all! Here is a poem.

Harry fights evil.
He really doesn't mean to.
He runs into trouble
Though he never mumbles.
Harry hears his mother's cry;
Harry can't help but try.
Voldemort's secret may soon be solved
If Harry ever finishes him off.
Harry duels away through the night,
He works his butt off through the fight.
   Alas, Voldemort disappears,
   And Harry's left with cold wet ears.
Harry, Harry, he never learns,
Harry, Harry, you'll soon be burned.
         (Malfoy says this.)
Harry, Harry, we were so worried,
Harry, Harry, we missed you so,
Harry, Harry, get up and hurry
For Dumbledore will soon show.
         (Hermione says that, of course!)
Harry, Harry, what was it like?
Harry, Harry, was it last night?

Harry, Harry, why didn't you come get me?
Harry, Harry, what do you see?
        (Ron says this.)
Harry stared into outer space;
Harry noticed that something was out of place.

∗

Eleanor, *Thornton-Cleveleys, Lancashire, England, 11 years old*

I wrote a poem about the Harry Potter books because I like
them so much!

I've never read a book like this one before,
I'm certain it's got a pretty good score.
It's witty, it's imaginative, I can't think of a better word,
I don't think there's a better book that's ever occurred.
Harry's so brave but maybe not attractive,
Hagrid is a softy, how could you sack him?
Ron is a sarcastic so-and-so,
Ask Hermione a quiz question, she's bound to know!
So far every book in the collection is better than the last,
So when J. K. Rowling writes the very last book it's certain to be
    a blast!

9 ✴

Letters from the Classroom:

Harry Potter in Our Schools

More and more teachers are including the Harry Potter books as part of their reading programs. Many of you children wrote us that you first discovered the joys of Hogwarts in your own schools.

Some teachers found that their pupils were so excited about the books that they assigned them to write letters sharing their thoughts and feelings. The children expressed their ideas and imaginings in letters to us (the producers of the book *We Love Harry Potter!*), to the characters created by J. K. Rowling, and to J. K. Rowling herself. The teachers sent these letters to us, and here they are.

From Mrs. Danielle Lyon's fifth grade class, Gulliver Academy, Coral Gables, Florida

My fifth grade students were inspired to write the following letters after I shared with them the book *We Love Harry Potter!* during a recent book talk in our classroom. The students have been eagerly reading and sharing comments, opinions, and beliefs about the Harry Potter series.

It is with great pride that I have watched them laugh and cry and become truly involved with books. Some of them have been turned on to reading for the very first time because of a little boy named Harry. For this I am very grateful!

Mrs. Danielle Lyon

✳

Dear Harry Potter,

I would just like to say that I can sometimes relate to the problems you have. It was very unfair of the Dursleys to keep you in the closet; it must have been creepy. It must have been freaky when Hagrid came to the Dursleys' house and told you you were a wizard. Is Dudley really mean to you? When you leave their house do you think you'll miss him? You have really inspired me to be happy even if I am down! Are you ever sad? Is Dudley ever nice to you? I hope so, because you sound like a very nice boy. Even though I am a girl, you are my role model, not as a wizard but as a person.

Carly

∗

Dear Hagrid,

Why can't you use magic on the Muggles? There must be a spell to make them forget what they saw. Did you ever go to college? How big is your bike?

Karl

∗

Dear Harry Potter,

When you fought Tom Riddle, you should've had Ron's wand. What if Mr. Dumbledore's bird [the phoenix Fawkes] never came? If you died, would you become best friends with Moaning Myrtle? When Percy came and Ginny needed to talk to you, you should've chased after her!

Andrea

∗

Dear Harry Potter,

You always get in a lot of trouble and always luck out. How do you do it? Where did you buy your owl? Because I really liked it. Is the wizard money really gold? How much money do you have?

Beau

∗

Dear Ron Weasley,

I wouldn't feel too bad about not getting anything new. I always have to wear the old clothes of my brothers, and I hardly ever get anything new to play with. I get Eric's old Legos and Bill's old clothes. So don't think you're the only one who doesn't get anything new.

Matthew

∗

Dear Hagrid,

Can I ask you a question? Why and who wanted Harry to play Quidditch and who wanted him to play for the team, and why and who wanted Harry to go to Hogwarts?

Roman

➜ *Note: We would all like to know the answers to those questions! We can only suppose that J. K. Rowling's wizards were also historians who kept track of Harry and arranged for him to go to Hogwarts and play Quidditch, like his father, when he was old enough.*

∗

Dear Harry Potter,

I think you are very brave. You were way too easy on Dudley. I would have killed him if he did those things to me.

Your adventures are a little fake. But that's not the worst part; your hair is disgusting. Buy a brush and brush it.

Julian

∗

Dear Harry Potter,

Congratulations on your Quidditch match. How jealous was Draco?

Justin

∗

Dear Harry Potter,

To me, you are a superhero. I really admire how you aren't afraid of anything. I can't believe how you survived so many years with the Dursleys.

Stephanie

∗

Dear Harry Potter,

I have not read any of your books. I still don't want to. Everybody says you are great. Maybe the movie will be more interesting.

Do you think you will have any siblings? Or maybe an evil twin? Or will you have a magical camera that turns people invisible? I'm not really interested in the books. But I can't wait to see what you will think of next.

Natasha

∗

Dear Harry Potter,
The reason I am writing to you is because your book is wonderful. It has very exciting moments, especially when they are in a very small shelter and they give Harry a little place on the floor to sleep and then they hear a knock on the door!

Andres

∗

Dear Harry Potter,
I love your books so much. They're so adventurous and enjoyable. Now don't think I'm a reading freak or anything, okay? Just because I love to read doesn't mean I'm a reading freak. Where I used to live, in Bangkok, Thailand, everyone loves your books, especially the kids and librarians in my old school. You should visit Bangkok sometime. It's fun there.

Natalie

∗

Dear Harry Potter,
I was wondering where you got the courage to fight He-Who-Must-Not-Be-Named. And about those exams; are they harder than Muggle exams? Does wizard food taste better than Muggle food?

Amelia

∗

Dear Hermione,
Why do you want to do so many subjects? Also, why do you always try to ruin things? Like when Harry was using the secret pas-

sages. I thought that you would tell on Harry. Then I can't believe that you said something about the Firebolt. I thought Harry would never get it back.

Tyler

∗

Dear Hermione,

How do you get yourself into all of that trouble when you are so smart? I have a recipe for butterbeer. It is: Take butterscotch hard candy and let it sit in frozen beer until it defrosts and then put it in the microwave. Add some sugar and, yum-yum! butterbeer. What do you think?

Cara

∗

Dear Dumbledore,

I was wondering how you became the headmaster at Hogwarts. I also want to know if you ever went face-to-face with Voldemort when you were a kid like Harry. How did you get that phoenix? The bird really is a lifesaver. I was thinking probably you will retire and Snape will take over.

Jorge

∗

Dear Editors of *We Love Harry Potter!*,

My favorite character is Hagrid. He is big and strong, but he seems like a very nice guy. I like to read the parts when he talks because his accent is fun to read. You feel like he is really talking to you. In the first book when he got mad at the Dursleys it was scary.

Melissa

∗

Dear Editors of *We Love Harry Potter!*,

I have an idea for the fifth Harry Potter book. Harry could have a secret evil twin brother. They would be identical twins. In the final book Harry would kill the evil one.

Frankie

*

Dear J. K. Rowling,

I think your Harry Potter books were pretty good. I think that you should write fifty more Harry Potter books, and each one would be ten times better. If you did do that, it would be awesome. If you don't do that, can you make a new series? This time you can write down notes on paper, not napkins.

Spencer

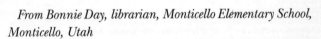

*

From Bonnie Day, librarian, Monticello Elementary School, Monticello, Utah

Our sixth grade classes have gotten so involved in and excited about the Harry Potter book series that they wanted to write letters to express this.

Bonnie Day

*

Dear Ms. Rowling,

In your first Harry Potter book I like how you made him sleep in a cupboard. What made you think of writing the Harry Potter books the way they are?

Whitney

*

Dear J. K. Rowling,

I read your first book last summer in about five days. A reader can really get into your books. In the third book, I thought Sirius Black was You-Know-Who in disguise.

How did you come up with all the names for creatures and people and the things at Hogwarts, like talking chess and the Sorcerer's Stone?

Kaitlyn

✱

Dear Miss Rowling,

Where and why did you come up with all of the sorcery in all the books? Well, I am going to say that if you hadn't written the Harry Potter books, then the people who read them would be bored.

Marissa

✱

Dear J. K. Rowling,

Last year I was not an active reader, and now this year my friends wanted me to read this book and I loved it and now all I want to do is read. Please write more books.

Kamry

✱

Dear Ms. Rowling,

Is there a special place where you write your books? Is there a boy who inspired you or reminds you of Harry Potter? When you first started writing, did you write sloppy and fast with a bunch of ideas, or did you write it down neatly in one big story? Do you have idea people or do you think of your ideas yourself?

Carly

✱

Dear Ms. Rowling,

I like the Harry Potter series because it's full of mystery and adventure, and the fantasy is, well . . . modern. The books keep you in suspense so you just can't put them down and they keep baffling you so you still are guessing all the time.

Krista

From Mrs. Duke's fourth/fifth grade, Paul A. Fisher Public School, Burlington, Ontario, Canada

✶

Dear Ms. Rowling,

I really love your books because they keep me in suspense. It's the first time I've ever been so interested in reading books. Because of your books I love reading. The only thing wrong with them is . . . I can't put them down.

Andrew, 9 years old

✶

Dear J. K. Rowling,

Your books are so interesting because of all the description. How did you think of these ideas? How did you think of the names of the characters? The names are so cool!

I like one-headed dogs rather than the three-headed dog because you don't have to take care of three heads.

Kelly, 10 years old

✶

Dear Ms. Rowling,

I think it's neat the chess people [in the first book] could come alive! It was also neat that the chess set was big enough that real people could stand on a square! But I don't think a chess game could be that short. And how did Ron know exactly what Harry and Hermione should be?

Katie

◆◆ *Note: We assume the chess game in the first book was short because Ron was in a hurry on account of their dangerous situation, and so he took a lot of risks. Ron probably assigned Harry and Hermione to be a bishop and a castle because in the game of chess those pieces can move around the board most easily and can cover each other's positions.*

*

Dear J. K. Rowling,
My friend Kelly is like Hermione because she always tries to get me to study for tests.

Jennifer, 9 years old

*

Dear J. K. Rowling,
In your fifth, sixth, or seventh book you should make a Nimbus 3000 and Harry gets it. I liked your books because there was so much description and I could picture Harry, Ron, and Hermione perfectly!

Dennis

*

Dear Ms. J. K. Rowling,
I think that you should make a dictionary of names, because some names I can't pronounce.
My mom and brother loved the books and so did I!

Jordan, 10 years old

*

Dear Mrs. Rowling,
I'm wondering, where do you get your ideas? Are they from your life and children you know? Where did you get the idea of Harry having a scar? Why is the scar in the shape of a lightning bolt?
I like the way you have suspense at the end of every page, because most authors have the suspense at the end of a chapter.

Nicole

•➔ *Note: The lightning bolt shape of Harry's scar is a symbol of the powerful shock of the spell Voldemort used to try to kill Harry when he was a baby, according to J. K. Rowling's books.*

∗

Dear Miss Rowling,

How old are you going to be when you stop writing stories?

Rebecca, 11 years old

∗

Dear J. K. Rowling,

My favorite character is Hermione because she is so funny and smart, and she always does and says whatever is on her mind.

Jenna, 10 years old

∗

Dear J. K. Rowling,

Harry Potter and the Sorcerer's Stone was hard to understand at the beginning because you had to introduce all the characters. In the middle I understood it more and it was an excellent book. I was really happy I read that book.

Kathryn

∗

Dear J. K. Rowling,

I liked the first book, but you could've added a bit more action. If I played Quidditch I'd be a Chaser, because if I was a Beater I might hit somebody and I'd feel guilty.

Daniel, 10 years old

∗

Dear Ms. Rowling,

I thought that your first book was so amazing because of the describing words and the similes. If I could play Quidditch I would be a Seeker because I like to go really fast straight down.

Kelly

From Mr. Kalen Marquis's class, Kanaka Creek Elementary School, Maple Ridge, British Columbia

★

Dear Harry,

I would like to try Every Flavor Beans. I would like to get mint, strawberry, or raspberry. I would not like to get guts.

Duncan, 8 years old

★

Dear J. K. Rowling,

I wish the Invisibility Cloak was real. If I knew Nicolas Flamel, I would ask him to make the Philosopher's Stone* again.

Kaitlyn, 8 years old

★

Dear Harry,

I remember the time Hermione put a spell on Neville, and he froze face-flat on the ground. I think that would hurt.

Michael, 8 years old

★

Dear Harry Potter,

I like when all the letters to Harry shoot out [of the Dursleys' kitchen fireplace] like a machine gun in the first book. Who's on the back of the first book? I think it's Professor Dumbledore.

Steven, 8 years old

➤ *Note: A number of children have asked about the identity of the mysterious old man on the back of the first book's jacket. The most likely answer, as Steven suggests, is Dumbledore, who is the only ancient wizard we actually meet (we don't meet Nicolas Flamel face-to-face). The figure on the book jacket has Dumbledore's long silver beard and half-moon glasses.*

*Called the Sorcerer's Stone in the U.S. version of the books.

∗

Dear Hermione,

I think you are a great actor. You are my favorite character. It is amazing when you find out which bottle to drink, in the first book.

Heather

∗

Dear Harry Potter,

The Dursleys shouldn't treat you like dirt all the time. I would try to turn Aunt Petunia into a rat and Uncle Vernon into a dandelion and Dudley into a pig (like what Hagrid tried to do but only got the pig tail).

I love myth, legend, and fantasy. When I grow up I'm going to be a princess and live in a castle.

Gracie, 8 years old

∗

Dear Ron,

I wonder what it's like to live in a burrow where trolls go walking through your garden every day? Why is Ginnie so shy?

Daniel, 8 years old

∗

Dear Ron,

In the sixth book, I hope that the Dursleys live in the closet that they made Harry live in. I hope Harry has a castle. I like reading exciting books!

Jeffrey, 9 years old

∗

Dear Voldemort,

In one of the next books, I wish that you could make the whole Dursley family go to the hospital. And put a worm in Dudley's drink.

Tyler

From L. F. Morgan's third grade class, Kanaka Creek Elementary School, Maple Ridge, British Columbia

My Grade 3 class is wild about Ms. Rowling's books, and, I think, their enthusiasm shows in their letters. Hope you enjoy their comments.

L. F. Morgan

*

Dear Hagrid,

I hope you didn't step on anybody. How old are you? Do you have any brothers or sisters? What color is your dragon? I wish I had one. Does your dragon have any friends?

Brent, 8 years old

*

Dear J. K. Rowling,

I'd like to know how big is Hagrid. Because I'm not that big. Why is Hagrid so big? I would make him medium-sized. Everyone in the school is probably nicer than Voldemort.

Kyle, 8 years old

*

Dear J. K. Rowling,

When Hagrid got Fang, did he like him right away or did he have to wait until he did something good?

Jordan, 8 years old

*

Dear Harry,

Draco Malfoy seems as bad and mean as Voldemort. I have a pet named O.J., but he's a dog, not an owl. I am glad that I don't sleep at school, like you.

Sam, 8 years old

➤ *Note: Sam probably means he's glad he doesn't go to a boarding school.*

*

Dear Harry Potter,

Where were you born? I was born in Surrey Memorial Hospital. In the middle of the night, I dream about you.

Brittany, 8 years old

*

Dear J. K. Rowling,

How do you make a Harry Potter story into a book?

Michael, 9 years old

*

Dear Ron,

Is your house on the Moon? I think Harry will have a better time there. Dudley cannot bug him there.

Hailey, 8 years old

*

Dear J. K. Rowling,

I really like your stories. I want to know if Harry is real. Do you draw pictures? I want to be an artist when I grow up.

My teacher is reading the Harry Potter books to us. I really like the part [in the first book] when Harry stuck the wand up the troll's nose and when it came out it had boogers all over it. The kids laughed their heads off.

If I had powers I would make the teacher only think of fun and not work.

Samara, 8 years old

*

Dear Harry,

If I had an owl, I would make it do my homework. For example, spelling tests and math.

Jason, 8 years old

*

Dear Harry Potter,

I wish I was magical, too, so I could turn the teacher into a frog. I like how you sneak out at night. I thought it was funny when you pretended to do magic and freaked out Dudley.

Casandra, 8 years old

From Ms. Carmen Estevez, who teaches English as a second language to schoolchildren in Madrid, Spain. Here is a letter from Ms. Estevez and two from her students.

Almost right after I started hearing about Harry Potter, he hit the newspapers here. The kids and I have been boning up on his background and that of his "mother," J. K. Rowling. It's a wonderful success story. What I read about her makes me want to know her.

Both Victoria and Emily are wonderful students, and they are charming, good-humored, intelligent children. Both of them speak English quite well. I would love to say that they learned it all from me but that is not true. However, I think I have had a little to do with their success.

When I read the first Harry Potter book, I was reminded of Victoria every time Hermione appeared on the scene. Victoria thinks Hermione is a great deal like her, too.

Ms. Carmen Estevez

★

I like Harry Potter because he is the boy we all have in ourselves and he shows us the way out of the routine. I like Ron and his family because they represent making an effort to succeed without having money. Hermione is my reflection. I like Dumbledore because he is the father we all want, very wise and benevolent.

Neat things about the magic are: the food that never ends, the photos where the people move, the cape that makes you invisible. I love the food they have. Just thinking about Chocolate Frogs, my mouth starts watering, and those Every Flavor Beans are a really ingenious invention.

The scariest thing about the first book was the perfect way they described the resurrection of Lord Voldemort, because the adjectives were so exhaustive* that the situation appeared to be real.

I would like to play Quidditch as a hunter of the Quaffle.

I can avoid becoming a Muggle by escaping from this real world by reading these books, or doing magic tricks, or just inventing my own stories. I think the funniest thing about being a wizard is that you can change the world with your hands.

I dislike the Dursleys because they are a typical rich family whose only dream is to be admired by high society, and Snape because he doesn't have any enthusiasm for doing his job as a teacher.

A possible future story could be about the Dursleys, who would start being very kind to Harry but the truth is that they have been paid to do so by Malfoy's father whose only interest is to destroy Harry. Another possible story idea could be that the Muggle world would become too much involved in the magic world so it

---

*"Exhaustive" means "in complete detail."

would be in danger of destruction by the magic, but there would be Harry to save the situation.

Victoria

*

I like Harry and his friends because they are so adventurous. You are never bored.

I think Harry's adventures are scary because there is so much mystery. I like it because there are chases and secret passages. I love Quidditch. If I had a broomstick, I would pay attention to the rules. I wouldn't play my own version if the majority didn't want to, but if I could make the rules I'd say that you couldn't fight. If you do you will be expelled. And the players must change if they are tired.

Well, if I'm to be sincere, I have to say I hate the kind of food they eat, but the mixtures are interesting. I escape being a Muggle by believing in the magic, and by thinking that if everybody had it, that would be fantastic.

I solved the puzzles in the first book. I thought about it for a while, and when I had the answer I checked the book to see if the answer was correct. I think Hagrid might be a little bit more serious-minded, but I don't care that much about it. I think that in the next book Harry will fall in love with someone.

Emilia

10 ✴

Club Notes:

International News from Harry Potter Fan Clubs

Maybe it's because Gryffindor, Ravenclaw, Hufflepuff, and Slytherin—the houses at Hogwarts—seem like competing clubs. Or because the "gang"—Harry, Ron, Hermione, Neville, Hagrid, and their friends—make up a little society of their own, a society that we readers feel we belong to. Or maybe Harry Potter fans just like to meet and talk to each other. Whatever the reason, Harry Potter Clubs, made up of children of different ages, have sprung up all over the world! Here are reports from some of them.

*

Charlotte, *Ellerstadt, Germany, 13 years old*

I read all the Harry Potter books in German and the first and second ones in English. Now I'm starting the third. (Not easy reading but a good exercise!) In some ways, I'm really like Hermione. My brother is a Harry Potter fan, too. I'm in a Harry Potter fan club.

There are many Harry Potter fans in our class. For example, my friend Caroline: a year ago, she was reading nothing but love stories (bleargh!) but now she's nearly as "Potter-mad" as I am.

At our last Harry Potter fan club party, two girls had made

some Every Flavor Beans. I got a sugar one, thank goodness! I was dressed up as Harry. The rest were: another Harry, two Hermiones, Penelope, Fred Weasley, Lockhart, and Ginny. It was fun. We ran through the streets and asked people to buy some Every Flavor Beans. Or we asked them for the way to Diagon Alley. ("Diagon Alley? Nay, there ain't no Diagon Alley here.") We had great fun with Lockhart ("Ooh, how nice I am! Did I tell you the story about how I killed the Wagga Wagga Werewolf?") and Penelope ("I'll take fifty points from Gryffindor!").

About the books. Harry is my favorite. I also like Ron; I liked it when the Weasleys got the prize from the *Daily Prophet*. They really deserved it. Hermione is nice and very clever; she reads as much as me. Hagrid is really great; he is very big (like me! I'm the biggest pupil in our class, and that's not always nice) and as animal mad as my best friend who has fifteen pets!

Dumbledore is wise, but sometimes quite childish (I mean the words he used at the beginning of Harry's first year at Hogwarts). He's much, *much* more interesting than our headmaster.

I'd like to have a pet owl. Instead, I've only got a fat cat, who sleeps, like Scabbers, all day.

✶

Steffani, *Roy, Utah*

My friends and I started a Harry Potter fan club. Jennifer is George and Brooke is Fred, the mischievous twins. I am Malfoy.

The Harry Potter books teach you something that other books can't. Every time I read them I feel like I'm there.

✶

Shelley, *Lemington Spa, Warwickshire, England, 9 years old*

I got the first Harry Potter book when I was seven. I asked my teacher, Miss Henshaw, if she would read it. She loves the books. Arthur, Arjun, Gabriel, and I made a Harry Potter Club. I'm going to get Adam, my brother, to read the books.

I can't wait until I'm ten. I might get to go to Hogwarts. I've been to King's Cross Station.

➤➤ *Note: In J. K. Rowling's books, Harry and his friends board the train to Hogwarts at King's Cross Station.*

From the Harry Potter fan club at Norfolk Collegiate School, Norfolk, Virginia

★

Jana, *9 years old*

I really enjoy the Harry Potter books. In fact, they're even better than TV! They're my favorite books.

My school library has a Harry Potter fan club. I have a golden robe. I am in Ravenclaw although I wanted to be in Gryffindor—so did everyone else. My friend Meghan (the spell-checker thinks her name is Moony) is in Gryffindor.

★

Erica, *10 years old*

My mother says I am ten years old going on twenty. I have one dog and a four-year-old sister. I am in the unofficial Harry Potter fan club at my school, because I love the Harry Potter books.

Sometimes I lie on my bed and read them, pretending I am a witch or a sorceress in a far-off land, attending Hogwarts. Now I can't wait to see what kind of adventures Harry has in the next book.

★

Megan, *8 years old*

I am in the fourth grade. I skipped first grade and never went to preschool. I really like the first book, *Harry Potter and the Sor-*

cerer's Stone. It was the best book of them all. I have read all the books and really enjoyed them all.

*

Carolyn

The Harry Potter books are my favorite books in the world. I read them over and over again. Whenever I can't find a book to read, I read a Harry Potter book.

I can't wait for the next book to come out. I'm dying to get my hands on it. I am usually patient but these books are so good I can barely wait!

*

Kelsey, *11 years old*

I am involved in an unofficial Harry Potter club supervised by our librarian, Mrs. Dryer. We are doing things such as making wands, creating artwork, exploring the Internet, and best of all playing Quidditch.

*

Berkley, *11 years old*

I really like the Harry Potter books. I like reading about Harry, Hermione, Ron, and the other characters. Each of the books is more exciting than the last.

In our Harry Potter fan club we are making wands and practicing spells, and at the very end we are going to have a big Quidditch match. Not flying, of course. I heard that there will be a Harry Potter movie. I would probably like the movie, but I think I would like the books even better.

★

Kassie, *9 years old*

I am in the Harry Potter club at school. We get to pick robes. I picked a white robe. We also paint wands and decorate them. We make green cookies and play Quidditch.

★

Chris, *10 years old*

If I were to make up my own character for a Harry Potter book, I would probably make up an apprentice to Voldemort. He would guard him at all times and when he was in need of help. I wonder if that apprentice wouldn't come in handy? I got kind of suspicious about how Voldemort by himself could be so powerful, if you know what I mean.

The following letters were sent by Debra Mansell, adviser to the Harry Potter Club at Pomfret Community School, Pomfret Center, Connecticut

★

Anneliese, *7½ years old*

I had a dream in which a bunch of dinosaurs were chasing Harry when he had a broken leg. I hope Crookshanks will be in the next book.

★

Ethan, *9 years old*

I liked the second book because it had a mystery on every page.

∗

Charlie, *11 years old*

Harry is so cool. So valiant, brave, and caring he is. I would love to go to Hogwarts. I could use a little magic in my life.

∗

Karen, *8 years old*

I wish the publishers of the Harry Potter books would just get a move on and go quicker. I like Harry Potter as much as Britney Spears. J. K. Rowling should write about Ron Weasley and the silver unicorn.

∗

Ashley, *10 years old*

I think one day Harry and Hermione will fall in love. Because of the time when he saved her from the troll. And Hermione risked her reputation to save Harry and Ron from getting in trouble.

In my school there is a club where we Harry Potter lovers gather. We talk and learn things like juggling and magic tricks, and we even thought of a way to play Quidditch. We have a lot of fun and I love it.

∗

Mike, *9 years old*

My favorite is the second book. I like the part when blood spurts out of the diary written by Tom Marvolo Riddle. I liked the part when Voldemort changed the letters. I switched around the letters in that name and got Lord Voldemort.

Hey, I forgot to tell you that I am part of a Harry Potter club at school. We play Quidditch, but I can't reveal how we play it.

11

Letters from Grown-ups:

The Views of Adult Readers

Many of you told us that your parents, grandparents, other relatives, and teachers love reading the Harry Potter books. There are also many grown-up Harry Potter fans who don't even have children (or whose children are adults themselves).

In fact, there are so many grown-ups interested in reading the books that their publisher considered issuing them with special jackets without the illustrations for any adults who might feel embarrassed to be seen reading children's fiction!

Grown-ups find the Harry Potter books just as gripping and suspenseful as children do. They don't identify with the characters as closely, not being children themselves, but they do remember what it was like when they were young. The adult readers are often people who show great respect for kids' minds and imaginations.

Here are letters from some adult admirers of Harry Potter who love the books just as much as younger folk do.

★

Dear friends at Hogwarts,

My wife asked me a while back to read a children's book called *Harry Potter and the Sorcerer's Stone*. Being twenty-one years old, I was in no hurry to read it, nor was I keen on the idea of reading any children's book. Then she went on a trip to Illinois with our son, then four months old. I finished my other book the day they left. The next day I very reluctantly picked up *Harry Potter*. Listlessly, I ran through the first few pages, and that was that; I was permanently sucked into the world of Harry Potter. I couldn't put it down.

I had to work while my wife was away, and I also had to pack and clean house because we were moving to Illinois, you see, and I had very little time to read. So I read the book mostly on breaks at work. Still, with minimal time to read, I polished it off in two days.

Then I went nuts! I knew my wife had the other Harry Potter books, but I didn't know where they were—packed away in some box, buried under a mountain of moving mess? I called her to see if she could help narrow down the search. Finally, several days later, I found them. That day I was unable to read them, but the following day it snowed.

That may not sound weird to you, but here in sunny South Carolina, snow is as rare as, well, Snape handing out sweets. Everything was closed. With nothing else to do, I sat down to read book two. A few hours later, I realized I had read both of the other books. Then panic set in; now what was I going to do? No more Harry Potter!

The next day I ran to the bookstore to find when the next book would be released. July! Five months away! I ran around the bookstore and saw *We Love Harry Potter!* A reprieve! I bought it, and in a day, that too had gone to feed my insatiable Harry Potter appetite.

I cannot tell you how wonderful these books are. The characters are so real. They have the same emotions as we have here in the Muggle world. They, Harry and his friends, experience all the things I went through when I was in school. I just wish I had experienced them at Hogwarts. I think it's wonderful that the books let children see magic in a positive way. They let them have a bit of magic in their lives. The potential that children have when they open their minds is tremendous, and that's what I see Harry Potter doing. He lets people into his world and shows them how wonderful life can be; indeed, how magical it can be. I am appalled to see some educational and religious institutions trying to take these books off the shelves. These books encourage kids to read! In a day and age when video games and movies are all that kids are usually interested in, they want to take away the one book kids pick up on their own!

J. K. Rowling has done something wonderful. She not only invited us to join in Harry's adventures at Hogwarts, she also opened the door to letting kids and adults see what other fantastic worlds are out there to explore. I eagerly await her next Harry Potter books, and I can assure her that she has one more advocate of her great books. I intend to start my child's reading experience with them. Talk about a bedtime story!

I leave you with the wise words that the great Albus Dumbledore left to me when I started my adventure:

Nitwit! Blubber! Oddment! Tweak!

(Next time I write I'll try to send it by owl!)

Dale Beatty, parent
Greenville, South Carolina

✳

Dear Sirs,

Wow! I've just read *Harry Potter and the Goblet of Fire*!

I am a thirty-two-year-old mum of two boys and had no idea what the books were about. When my friend said she'd read them, my immediate reaction was, "But they're kids' books, aren't they?"

Well, I have to say that once I opened the first book I was well and truly hooked. I devoured the first three books and was outside my local bookstore an hour before it opened waiting for the fourth book!

I was very lucky indeed to get my book signed by Ms. Rowling on July 9. My husband is a railway buff and found out that Taw Valley, the steam train painted as "the Hogwarts Express," was staying overnight at Crewe station. So I set my alarm and waited at 8:30 A.M. on a cold, drizzly platform for a glimpse of my heroine. There were only six railway enthusiasts (there to see the train) and a little boy with his dad and myself. We waited by the old carriages but did not see Jo Rowling. Her press agent took our books and had them signed by her. I was on cloud nine all week! I took lots of photos of "the Hogwarts Express" and plan to put them in the Harry Potter scrapbook I am compiling. I have lots of newspaper cuttings and magazine interviews. I have entitled my scrapbook, "Muggle Adventures in Potterland."

I have now converted my husband. As soon as we came home from seeing "the Hogwarts Express" he picked up the first book and is now on the fourth.

I recommend *Harry Potter* to anyone who'll listen! I now have a shop promotional picture of Harry on his Firebolt zooming across my bedroom.

Andrea Golden-Hann
Cheshire, England

★

Dear Ms. Moore,

Thank you for writing *We Love Harry Potter!* It's great to hear that so many kids are pumped up about Harry, Hermione, Hagrid, and all the other wizards, Muggles, and creatures.

I used to work as a library assistant at the Kent Library in Washington State. I read the first book after hearing about all the parents who objected to it (I wanted to see what the fuss was about).

I've read the first four books and can't wait for the next three (or more). I can't really add anything that hasn't been said in

Chapter 5 of your book ("What Grown-ups Say About the Harry Potter Books") except that it's about time someone wrote *to* children instead of *down* to them.

Many grown-ups don't have a clue how smart kids are. While we should allow them their childhood, we should respect and nurture them. J. K. Rowling does all that and more. I look forward, rather impatiently, to her next Harry Potter book!

Lois J. Cuffin
Grayland, Washington

*

Dear All,

I have just finished reading *We Love Harry Potter!* I am so glad that so many people love him as much as I do! In fact, I love him so much that I have decided to do my whole dissertation in my final year at university on what it is about Harry Potter that children and adults find so appealing.

Tracy Pick
Essex, England

12 ✺

Cryptolog's Spelling Bees:

Outwit the Wizard and Break
His Spell on These Words

A clever but greedy wizard named Cryptolog plans to hoard the hidden power of language to gain power over all other wizards and to prevent readers of the Harry Potter books from learning his secrets. He has sent forth his swarm of Spelling Bees to cast a scrambling charm over some important words that were used in *Harry Potter and the Goblet of Fire*, so that no one else can recognize them. Reverse the charm by changing around the letters, and the words are yours!

1. Rommey
2. Guntrailar
3. Feetunor
4. Nittidye
5. Gaulibar
6. Brayuncil
7. Nightuna
8. Odorborfal
9. Rockenbriskeck
10. Sourbistoe
11. Spasmt
12. Dearnil
13. Braidtie
14. Pourra
15. Muppink
16. Huxadeets
17. Jaspama
18. Lottie
19. Feeprum
20. Tactocrenen
21. Ziddecanals
22. Mattaplenerem
23. Hussiteman
24. Tricanus

25. Glentad
26. Dropture
27. Dosethane

28. Griffoneer
29. Ripsed
30. Pusyfet

ANSWERS:

1. *Memory*
2. *Triangular*
3. *Fourteen*
4. *Identity*
5. *Bulgaria*
6. *Incurably*
7. *Haunting*
8. *Floorboard*
9. *Knickerbockers*
10. *Boisterous*
11. *Stamps*
12. *Ireland*
13. *Diatribe*
14. *Uproar*
15. *Pumpkin*

16. *Exhausted*
17. *Pajamas*
18. *Toilet*
19. *Perfume*
20. *Concentrate*
21. *Scandalized*
22. *Temperamental*
23. *Enthusiasm*
24. *Curtains*
25. *Tangled*
26. *Protrude*
27. *Headstone*
28. *Forefinger*
29. *Spider*
30. *Stupefy*

13 ✵

Crafty Crossword:

*Wave Your Magic Word-Wand Across
and Down to Unlock the Mysteries of This
Puzzle's Clues*

Y ou will need some wizard words and some perfectly ordinary everyday words to fill in the blanks, but if you use your magical imagination you will be able to complete the crisscrossing threads of this puzzle and weave a mystical text-ile!

1	2	3	4			5	6	7	8
9						10			
11						12			
13				14				15	
16					17		18		
		19			20				
21	22								
23							24	25	26
27		28	29				30		
31							32		

ACROSS

1. A witch uses one to sweep the sky
5. What even wizards have to do until they drop
9. A substance that grows mysteriously in your pocket
10. The bottoms of panthers' feet
11. What good little boys and girls get on the head (ugh!)
12. Stirs another toad, eyeball, or root into the pot
13. A finished piece of pottery
15. Lowest officer's rank in the army (abbreviation)
16. Rely on what you've studied
17. "Oh, dear, that's very, ____ strange!"
19. Initials for "the Movie Capital of America"
20. Ancient poem of praise
21. Nothing, in Latin
23. Press this switch if you don't want to be "off"
24. The bottom-most part of a piece of furniture
27. What the Southeast-Asian land of Myanmar was once called
30. It cleans even the uncleanable
31. Another name for the upper air, or a gas that makes you sleepy
32. Although

DOWN

1. An evil kind of magic
2. Grow up and become good-tasting
3. Doing so well you can't stop!
4. A Canadian Indian tribe and a city named for them
5. Set a certain distance apart
6. Ate or owned
7. How wizard lore strikes ordinary people
8. A person with a secret might whisper this in your ear
14. What elephants contribute to piano keys
18. Truly
21. What one person may stick into another person's business
22. If you are not out of a game, then you are ____ ____.

25. Take a look at
26. British slang for a person who's disliked (alternative spell-ing)
28. "That's it!"
29. The one most important in my life

¹B	²R	³O	⁴O	M		⁵S	⁶H	⁷O	⁸P
⁹L	I	N	T			¹⁰P	A	D	S
¹¹A	P	A	T			¹²A	D	D	S
¹³C	E	R	A	M	¹⁴I	C		¹⁵L	T
¹⁶K	N	O	W		¹⁷V	E	¹⁸R	Y	
		¹⁹L	A		²⁰O	D	E		
²¹N	²²I	L			R		A		
²³O	N				Y		²⁴L	²⁵E	²⁶G
²⁷S	I	²⁸A	²⁹M				³⁰L	Y	E
³¹E	T	H	E	R			³²Y	E	T

Answer to the Crafty Crossword

14 ✴

Myths and Legends:

Classic Folklore for Harry Potter Fans

In J. K. Rowling's books, the names of many characters and creatures come from ancient stories that are called myths or legends. Sometimes, she combines myths and invents a new word or idea that means something even more exciting than the originals. For instance, the most evil character in her books ("You-Know-Who") acts like a vampire, a snake, and a ghost at different times.

In *Harry Potter and the Goblet of Fire*, there are many new words and characters that can be traced back to ancient lore. See if you can match up some of the following legendary creatures, characters, objects, and practices with those in the Harry Potter books.

Alchemy. The study of mixing different substances, usually metal, in an attempt to make gold or the "elixir of life." Early alchemists were Greeks living in Egypt. Their knowledge spread to Europe during the Middle Ages. They tried to change one substance into another and searched for the philosopher's stone, which they believed would make the changing process easier.

Basilisk. Also called the cockatrice, the basilisk emerges from the egg of a cock (a *male* chicken!) hatched under toads or snakes.

With its stare, the basilisk can kill any creature except a weasel. Those who hunted the basilisk used a mirror to turn its lethal stare back onto its owner. The basilisk was first mentioned by the ancient Greeks and Romans.

Dragon. These huge fire-breathing reptiles appear in the myths of many countries. In an ancient Babylonian legend, the dragon Tiamat gave birth to the first gods, who created the first humans. The Egyptian dragon Apep tried to overthrow the sun god, Ra. In China, there were said to be many kinds of dragons, most of them friendly. So the dragon represented good fortune and prosperity to the Chinese. The fire-breathing monster Leviathan is recorded in the book of Job, in the Bible. The first dragon slain in the Western world was Python, killed by the Greek god Apollo. On one of his adventures, Hercules slew the dragon Ladon, which guarded the golden apples of the goddess Hera. According to the Norse myths, the dragon Nidhogg, "the fearsome biter," lived in Niflheim, the Norse underground. Alexander the Great was said to be the son of a dragon. In the late Middle Ages, knights like St. George were expected to proved their valor by rescuing fair maidens from dragons.

Druids. An ancient order of priests and sorcerers in Britain, Ireland, and Gaul (ancient France), who worshipped nature gods and believed in reincarnation. They held services in circles of stones, amid groves of oak trees, and at holy wells and river sources; and they sometimes sacrificed animals and even humans. They collected the mistletoe that grew on certain oak trees, during certain phases of the moon, and used it in their rituals. Their emblem was a snake's egg. Their two great festivals were Beltane, in spring, and Samhain, at Halloween. The Druids studied the stars and the Earth, as well as ethics and poetry. They settled disputes, set up a legal system, and preserved the ancient Celtic culture which they taught to the young. The time of the Druids' greatest power was around 2000 B.C., and the ancient monument of Stonehenge is thought to have been one of their temples. The Druids were finally conquered by the Romans. Julius Caesar greatly admired their wisdom and knowledge.

Elves. In Norse mythology, there were two kinds of elves. The light elves were kind and looked like beautiful children. The dark elves were ugly, hated the sun, and lived in caves. They were skilled craftsmen. In old Ireland, the brownies were tiny elves who hung around people's houses, doing chores for them in exchange for food and clothing.

Flying horse. According to Greek myth, when Perseus beheaded the fearful monster Medusa, from its blood sprang the winged horse Pegasus. Another hero, Bellerophon, tried to ride Pegasus up into the heavens, but was thrown off. Pegasus remained in the skies as a constellation.

Giant. Some of the giants of ancient Greek myth were only somewhat bigger than humans, such as the Cyclopes and Orion. But others were even bigger. When the giant Tityus fell down, his body covered nine acres! In Norse mythology, Thor camped out one night in what he thought was a castle, but in the morning he discovered that it was the glove of a giant called Skrymir. What he had taken to be a tower was actually the thumb of the glove.

Hippogriff. Among the legends of the ninth-century French king Charlemagne is the story of Bradamante. She was a woman warrior who freed her beloved Rogero from an evil enchanter who rode a hippogriff. Rogero then escaped on the enchanter's hippogriff, but did not know how to control the beast and so was carried off to further adventures. The hippogriff had the body of a horse and the head of an eagle, with claws and wings. It originated in the mythical northern land of Hyperborea in old Greek mythology. Rogero and Bradamante did find each other again, and lived happily ever after.

Merlin. An ancient Welsh poet, sometimes also called Taliesin. Merlin's father was not a mortal, and Merlin inherited his mystical powers. He could transform himself into any sort of creature, and was seen as a dwarf, a lady, a page (a noble's young servant), a dog, or a stag. Merlin was said to be responsible for bringing great stones from Ireland to be set up as Stonehenge on Salisbury Plain. According to the legends of King Arthur, Merlin united Arthur's parents, Uther and Igraine, and arranged the famous contest of the sword, Excalibur, in the stone. Because young Arthur was the only knight who could pull Excalibur out of the stone he was made king. Merlin fell in love with Vivien, one of the Ladies of the Lake who had guarded Excalibur, and who used his magical secrets to betray him. Merlin helped Arthur to conquer his foes and rule his country through magic. It was Merlin who created the Round Table for King Arthur's knights. He became Arthur's counselor, but went mad after seeing a terrible vision in the sky during a great battle and afterward disappeared from history.

Odin, the One-Eyed God. The Scandinavian god became all-knowing by drinking from the spring of Mimir, which cost him the loss of one eye. His other eye was the Sun. Odin was killed by the wolf-god Fenrir.

Phoenix. A beautiful, magical bird that eats incense and lives for five hundred years. When it dies, in a fragrant fire of spices, it gives birth to a young phoenix. Legends of the phoenix come from ancient Egypt and Assyria.

The Holy Grail. This legend combines an ancient pagan Celtic story of a magical cup or stone, with the history of the cup from which Jesus drank at the Last Supper. According to the legend, a follower of Jesus took the sacred cup to Europe, but then it disappeared. Once, during a feast at Camelot, it appeared to King Arthur and his knights amid a bright light with a clap of thunder, and they vowed to make a holy quest to find it. The cup could only be found by the bravest and purest of the knights.

Vampire. The vampire bat has lived on earth for thousands of years, but the legend of a human vampire arose in Eastern Europe sometime during the Middle Ages. The famous story of the vampire Dracula is based on a fifteenth-century Romanian named Vlad Tepes, also known as "Vlad the Impaler" for his brutal methods of war. "Dracula" means "son of Dracul." His father was called Vlad Dracul, because he belonged to the Order of the Dragon. (Dracul is the Romanian word for "dragon.") It was said that people who take their own lives, die violent deaths, or are banned by a religious group are likely to become vampires. A vampire is believed to shun mirrors, garlic, and the Christian cross, and can only be killed by driving a wooden stake through its heart.

Vila. A supernatural creature, like a fairy, who lives in mountains and woods and often appears in the form of a beautiful young woman. The legend originally came from Bulgaria.

Werewolf. An Old English word that means "man-wolf." In some old stories, people turn themselves into wolves by covering themselves with the skin of wolf or by drinking water left in a wolf's footprint. To force a werewolf to return to its human form, you can say aloud the werewolf's human name, strike it three times on the forehead, or make the sign of the cross.

Appendix: Other Books for Harry Potter Fans to Read

Novels and Nonfiction Books for Young Readers

Here are some books of fantasy and adventure fiction that you might enjoy.

The Secrets of Droon series, by Tony Abbott

Watership Down, by Richard Adams

Chronicles of Prydian series, by Lloyd Alexander

The Lost Years of Merlin series, by T. A. Barron

The Mists of Avalon, and its sequels *The Forest House* and *The Lady of Avalon,* by Marion Zimmer Bradley (for young adults)

The Dark Is Rising series *(Over Sea, Under Stone; The Dark Is Rising; Greenwitch; The Grey King; Silver on the Tree),* by Susan Cooper

Willie Wonka and the Chocolate Factory and *James and the Giant Peach,* by Roald Dahl

Half Magic, Knight's Castle, Magic by the Lake, and *The Time Garden* by Edward Eager

The Secret of Platform 13 and other books by Eva Ibbottson

The *Redwall* series, by Brian Jacques

The Phantom Tollbooth, by Norton Juster

A Wrinkle in Time, and the other books in *The Time Quartet (A Wind in the Door; A Swiftly Tilting Planet;* and *Many Waters),* by Madeleine L'Engle

The Chronicles of Narnia series *(The Lion, the Witch and the Wardrobe; Prince Caspian; The Voyage of the Dawn Treader; The Silver Chair; The Horse and His Boy; The Magician's Nephew;* and *The Last Battle),* by C. S. Lewis

Dragonsong, Dragonsinger, and *Dragondrums,* by Anne McCaffrey

Works of E. Nesbitt such as *Five Children and It; The Phoenix and the Carpet; The Story of the Amulet; The Enchanted Castle; The Story of the Treasure Seekers;* and *The Magic City.* (J. K. Rowling's favorite books when she was growing up.)

Works of Tamora Pierce

His Dark Material series *(The Golden Compass; The Subtle Knife; The Amber Spyglass),* by Philip Pullman

The Westing Game, by Ellen Raskin

Holes, by Louis Sachar

The Hobbit and *The Lord of the Rings* trilogy, by J.R.R. Tolkien

The Once and Future King, by T. H. White

Enchanted Forest Chronicles, by Patrice Wrede

Here are some books on myths and legends that young readers might enjoy.

101 Read-Aloud Celtic Myths and Legends, by Joan C. Verniero

Brewer's Dictionary of Phrase and Fable, by Ebenezer C. Brewer, et. al.

Bulfinch's Mythology, by Thomas Bulfinch

D'Aulaires' Book of Greek Myths, by Ingri and Edgar D'Aulaire

Dragons, by Peter Hogarth with Val Clery

Mythology, by Edith Hamilton

These booklists were compiled by the staff specializing in children's books at City Lights Bookstore in Sylva, North Carolina.

When we published *We Love Harry Potter! We'll Tell You Why,* we invited you to send us your comments, ideas, letters to characters in the Harry Potter books, and any other thoughts on the whole Hogwarts crew. You responded very enthusiastically, and many of your comments and drawings have been included in this book. We'd love to get more letters and drawings, especially about the most recently published J. K. Rowling book(s) in the Harry Potter series, and about the upcoming movie. Hopefully, you'll send us enough letters to make a third tribute book possible!

If you'd like to send us a letter, drawing, or anything else so we perhaps can publish all or part of it in another book, send it to:

Department JW, Editorial
St. Martin's Press
175 Fifth Avenue
New York, NY 10010

Please make sure to tell us your first and last name and age so we can include them if we use any of what you send us. Please also enclose a letter from your mom or dad saying it's okay for us to use what you're sending in the book. We look forward to hearing from you!